DE

PROFILES IN POWER

General Editor: Keith Robbins

DE GAULLE

Andrew Shennan

LONGMAN
London and New York

Longman Group UK Limited
Longman House, Burnt Mill,
Harlow, Essex CM20 2JE, England
and Associated Companies throughout the world.

*Published in the United States of America
by Longman Publishing, New York*

First published 1993

ISBN 0582 21881 0 CSD
ISBN 0582 00967 7 PPR

British Library Cataloguing-in-Publication Data

A catalogue record for this book is available from the British Library

Library of Congress Cataloguing-in-Publication Data

Shennan, Andrew
De Gaulle / Andrew Shennan.
p. cm. — (Profiles in power)
Includes bibliographical references and index.
ISBN 0-582-21881-0. – ISBN 0-582-00967-7 (pbk.)
1. Gaulle, Charles de, 1890–1970. 2. Presidents–France-
-Biography. 3. Generals–France–Biography. 4. France. Armée-
-Biography. 5. France–Politics and government–20th century.
I. Title. II. Series: Profiles in power (London, England)
DC420.S48 1993
944.083'6'092–dc20
[B]   92-46023
                                        CIP

Set 7P in 11/12 New Baskerville
Produced by Longman Singapore Publishers (Pte) Ltd
Printed in Singapore

CONTENTS

LIST OF MAPS

PREFACE

The American political scientist Stanley Hoffmann once remarked that there were really three de Gaulles. One was Charles de Gaulle the private man – the third of five children in a close-knit Catholic family of faded aristocracy, who married a woman from a northern bourgeois background, had three children of his own (the last born with Down's syndrome), and lived an uneventful and unimpeachably respectable family life. Although biographers and historians have uncovered a good deal about his early years, his upbringing, his intellectual development, and, later, his family life as a public figure, Charles remains a somewhat shadowy figure, partly because he was scrupulous about keeping his private life private, but perhaps also because he was as unexceptional as he appeared.

The second de Gaulle was the historic or, perhaps more accurately, mythic figure of General de Gaulle – the man who twice rescued his country from disaster and, in the process, took on a larger identity as the personification of eternal France. The essential point to understand about this persona is that it was not the fortuitous product of events; it was a premeditated self-creation. Long before he became a public figure, de Gaulle conceived a role for himself – that of a solitary, proud, and self-reliant 'man of character', who in a moment of dire emergency would rise from obscurity to save his country. In 1940 he played out this role. Thereafter, he deployed his extraordinary gifts as speaker and writer to perpetuate and refine the mythology of the General who literally became France.

This mythic figure has dominated scholarly perceptions

of de Gaulle. Scholars have been intrigued by the continual interplay between de Gaulle the writer and de Gaulle the actor, seduced by the granite-like consistency of his ideas and attitudes, intimidated by the superbly tendentious account of his career that he gave in his memoirs. They have generally assumed (not without justification) that most of de Gaulle's actions after 1940 were determined by this mythic persona which he had created and to which he himself referred in the third person.

Increasingly this mythic figure also dominates popular memories of him. In 1990 France commemorated the hundredth anniversary of his birth, the fiftieth anniversary of his wartime heroics, and the twentieth anniversary of his death. The scope and style of the commemoration showed very clearly that de Gaulle is no longer viewed as a political figure in the narrow sense. As General de Gaulle, he has entered the pantheon of great national heroes, where he ranks (according to a public opinion poll taken in 1990) ahead of Napoleon and behind only Charlemagne.

Apparently fading from memory is the third de Gaulle – de Gaulle the politician (much though he detested the word) who headed a provisional government in 1944–46, left office and entered opposition for more than a decade, and then returned to power in 1958, to serve for over ten years as the first president of the Fifth Republic. In spite of the consensual mythology of General de Gaulle the national saviour and liberator, de Gaulle the politician inevitably became, and came to be seen as, a partisan figure – not only because he took strong positions on political issues and came into conflict with other politicians, but because he was associated with a Gaullist movement which acquired a partisan identity in French politics.

This book is primarily concerned with the third de Gaulle. My aim is not to demythologize, since there is little point in demythologizing a person who always saw himself in mythic terms. Rather it is to distinguish, as far as is possible, the mythic from the political, and to present a critical interpretation of his political career in its various dimensions and phases. This interpretation rests on a simple premise which should be stated at the outset: contrary to Gaullist legend, the career of the politician cannot be understood solely by reference to the mythic figure of the General. The mythic identity was a starting-point for the political leader (a starting-point to which he constantly returned for inspiration and guidance), but only a starting-point. The hero of Gaullist legend, who found his ultimate expression in de Gaulle's own memoirs, was fully formed and virtually immutable from the moment that he entered history. The politician was neither fully formed nor immutable. Like all political figures, he changed and, in a certain sense, 'grew'. The long, complex, and incomplete process whereby de Gaulle took on a political identity without giving up a mythic identity is the subject of this book.

I am very grateful to Keith Robbins and Longman for giving me the opportunity to write this book; to Wellesley College, the libraries of the University of Massachusetts and Harvard University, and the staffs of Y's Kids and Sunnyside child care centres for making it possible for me to write it; and to Elizabeth Doherty, Steven Goldstein, Peter Morris, and Keith Robbins for making it better than it would otherwise have been. Any shortcomings that remain are entirely my own.

. . .

Note In the notes at the end of each chapter I have used the following abbreviations to refer to the two major published collections of de Gaulle's speeches and political papers:

DM De Gaulle C 1970 *Discours et messages* (5 vols). Plon, Paris
LNC De Gaulle C 1980–88 *Lettres, notes et carnets* (12 vols). Plon, Paris

FOR BETH

Chapter 1

1940: THE ASSUMPTION

'In each historic destiny, there is the moment when it all begins,' said the great writer and Gaullist André Malraux.[1] In Charles de Gaulle's case, it all began in 1940 amid the confusion and humiliation of France's defeat by Nazi Germany. On 5 June, as Hitler's army prepared to move on Paris, Prime Minister Paul Reynaud appointed de Gaulle Under-Secretary of State for National Defence. He held this post for less than a fortnight. On 16 June Reynaud resigned and turned the premiership over to Marshal Pétain, the victor of Verdun in the First World War but the leading advocate of an armistice with the Germans in 1940. The following day, recognizing that there was no prospect of a Pétain government supporting continued resistance, de Gaulle flew from Bordeaux to England. On the evening of 18 June he broadcast his celebrated 'appel' ('appeal') over the BBC. He told the French people that their army had been overwhelmed by the enemy's Blitzkrieg tactics but insisted that the defeat was reversible. The battle of France was only one battle in a world war. France still had at her disposal her own empire, all the resources of the British empire, and the industrial resources of the United States. He concluded:

> I, General de Gaulle, now in London, call on French officers and men who are on British soil or may reach it, with or without their arms; I call on engineers and skilled workers from the armament industry who are on British soil or may reach it, to make contact with me. Whatever happens, the flame of French resistance must not and shall not die out.[2]

1

This short broadcast of little more than three hundred words marked the real beginning of de Gaulle's political career and the birth of Gaullism. It was de Gaulle's first communication with the French people *en masse* (although not many of them heard it). It established de Gaulle's reputation as the first resister. Retrospectively, it came to define the political identity that he was to assume in the war years and, indeed, that he retained for the rest of his life – the identity of a solitary leader, who achieves greatness through a combination of his own strength of character, the failure of others, and the supreme distress of his country. In his memoirs de Gaulle did not bother to recall his emotions on being appointed Under-Secretary of State in a regime which he despised. But he did recollect his feelings on 18 June: 'I felt within myself one life coming to an end . . . At the age of 49, I was entering upon adventure, like a man whom destiny was casting outside all normal terms of reference.'[3]

. . .

Who was this tall, ungainly figure at the microphone? Those who had heard of Charles de Gaulle before 18 June 1940 – a sizeable number within political and military circles in Paris but few outside – were most likely to associate his name with the public campaign for a professional, motorized army that he had launched in the mid-1930s. The first biography of him – written in 1940–41 by Philippe Barrès – laid great stress on his prewar prescience about Blitzkrieg. Barrès' book contained an anecdote that – true or not – quickly established itself at the core of Gaullist legend. He reported that in 1934 he had talked with Ribbentrop and with the head of the Nazi tank corps, both of whom had inquired about the French expert in motorized warfare, Colonel de Gaulle.[4] At that time, Barrès himself had never heard of this French expert so admired in Germany.

Interestingly, this record was not something that de Gaulle himself stressed at the outset. He preferred to present himself as a providential figure, without any record whatsoever. When British officials asked him to provide a thumbnail sketch of himself for publicity purposes, he gave them the following:

2

I am a free Frenchman.
I believe in God and in the future of my fatherland.
I belong to no one. I have one and only one mission: to pursue the struggle for the liberation of my country.
I solemnly declare that I am not attached to any political party, nor connected to any politician whatsoever . . .
I have only one objective: to rescue France.[5]

Here, in characteristically liturgical style, were the dominant images of de Gaulle in 1940: a simple patriot, without political past or hidden ties, who had emerged into public life suddenly, 'as Minerva emerged from Jupiter's thigh',[6] as a result of national catastrophe. The implication was that there was no pre-history, just a sudden metamorphosis from Charles de Gaulle to General de Gaulle. To the Gaullists who witnessed it, the metamorphosis was almost miraculous.[7]

Biographers of de Gaulle have naturally felt an obligation to explain, if not to demythologize, the miracle. The purpose of the early chapters in most biographies is to show how 'the man of 18 June 1940' had been there all along. The traits that they tend to emphasize – because these were also the most striking characteristics of his behaviour in June 1940 – are his monumental self-assurance or belief in his own destiny and his relish for confrontation with misguided superiors.

Early instances of de Gaulle's self-assurance are innumerable. One is an essay that de Gaulle wrote as a fifteen-year-old schoolboy, in which he described a German invasion of France in 1931 and the emergence of a certain 'General de Gaulle' to lead the nation to salvation.[8] Another frequently cited incident occurred in the early 1920s, when de Gaulle was at the War College, where the army's top officers were trained. One day a fellow officer told de Gaulle that he was destined for great things. Instead of giving the sarcastic response that the officer had anticipated, de Gaulle replied quite seriously: 'Yes, I think so too.'[9]

Examples of de Gaulle's independent-minded temperament are equally legion. Again, some of the classic episodes took place at the War College, where de Gaulle clashed repeatedly with his instructors. In one famous incident during a debriefing at the end of the course, de Gaulle was confronted by the chief lecturer in general tactics, Colonel Moyrand. Moyrand had been exasperated by de Gaulle's unorthodox performance during the final exercises and attempted to show him up in front of his peers. 'Where are the supply trains of the left-hand regiment of your right-flank division?' De Gaulle turned to the officer who had been acting as his chief of staff. 'Chateauvieux, please answer.' 'I asked you, de Gaulle,' Moyrand interjected furiously. 'Mon colonel,' came the reply, 'you have entrusted me with the responsibilities of a corps commander. If I had to do my subordinates' jobs as well, I would not have my mind free to do my own properly. Chateauvieux, please answer the Colonel.'[10]

Similarly instructive about the young de Gaulle's capacity to stand his ground was the long saga of his collaboration and subsequent conflict with Philippe Pétain. Pétain had been de Gaulle's commanding officer in his first posting after military school in 1912 and had quickly formed a very high opinion of the young officer's talents. In the mid-1920s, he had brought de Gaulle into his cabinet and asked him to 'ghost' a book (then entitled *Le Soldat* and later published with the title *La France et son armée*), which was to appear under the Marshal's name. Subsequently, Pétain decided to involve other officers in the project, but de Gaulle objected. In 1928 the junior officer wrote a respectful but very firm letter to his powerful patron, explaining that the book was essentially his own and that, though he was willing to see it published under Pétain's name (provided that de Gaulle's contribution was duly noted in a preface), he was not willing to work with other authors. The letter testified both to his self-assurance and to the limits of his respect for hierarchy, when what he perceived as an important principle (i.e. the honouring of a commitment that Pétain had made to him) was at stake.[11] It was the beginning of a breach between the two men that widened over the succeeding decade and became official in 1938, when de Gaulle finally went ahead with the publication of his book.

This kind of evidence from de Gaulle's past, though inevitably tinged with retrospection, certainly helps to explain his actions in 1940 and afterwards. It is important, however, to see the anecdotes in their larger context. De Gaulle's career before 1940 was certainly not the smoothest or most conventional of military careers, but neither was it wholly out of the ordinary.

He had been born in 1890 into a deeply patriotic, monarchist family. On his father's side it was a family of writers, civil servants, and intellectuals; on his mother's side a family of pious northern bourgeois. After being educated at the Jesuit school where his father taught, he prepared for the entrance examination for the military school at Saint-Cyr. In 1909, on his first try, he was accepted. At Saint-Cyr he was an ambitious and successful cadet, who worked his way up the ranking to graduate thirteenth out of more than two hundred. With that record he could have had his pick of postings, but he opted to join the unfashionable infantry.

In the First World War, he fought with distinction, was wounded on three occasions, and spent the final thirty-two months of the war as a prisoner in Germany. Afterwards he served briefly in Poland, where he saw action against the Red Army. In 1921, on his return to France, he became a lecturer in military history at Saint-Cyr. Three years later, he published his first book, *Discord among the Enemy* (*La Discorde chez l'ennemi*), which he had worked on while a prisoner-of-war in Germany and in which he analysed the reasons for Germany's defeat in 1918. Also in 1924 he completed his two-year course at the War College, graduating with a grade of 'mention bien' – less distinguished than he or Pétain felt he deserved. After a brief posting to Mainz, he was recalled to Paris in 1925 to serve under Pétain at the Supreme War Council. In addition to commissioning him to write *Le Soldat*, the Marshal also arranged for his protégé to deliver three lectures at the War College before the very officers who had clashed with him two years earlier. The subject was the role of the leader, and not unnaturally many in the audience took a dim view of being lectured on this subject by Captain de Gaulle. After this brief controversy, de Gaulle returned to active service. In the autumn of 1927 he was promoted and took command of the 19th Light Infantry Battalion, based at Trier in Germany. Then in 1929 he was posted to Beirut to serve in the Army of the Levant.

At the end of 1931 he returned to Paris to serve in the

Secretariat of the Supreme Council for National Defence. Shortly afterwards he published his second book, *The Edge of the Sword* (*Le Fil de l'épée*), which was a revised and expanded version of his 1927 lectures on leadership. Although many of its precepts could be applied to the political realm, this long essay dealt primarily with military leadership. Its full significance only became appreciated in retrospect (i.e. after 1940), when readers saw that the 'man of character' whom the book depicted – a self-reliant, strong leader to whom his people rallied only in emergency – was, in fact, de Gaulle himself.

De Gaulle's career up to 1932 had not been wholly typical of a French officer's career: the literary dimension to it was somewhat unusual and in some quarters frowned upon; the 1927 lectures and the various other minor confrontations were atypical in an inherently conformist milieu. That said, it *had* been the career of a military officer, without political or public aspects. In spite of their evident concern with issues of statecraft, both his books had been aimed primarily at a military audience. The eight articles that he had written before 1933 had all been published in military journals. It is important to recognize this, in order to appreciate the significant change that took place in 1933 and 1934, with the publication of his views on motorized warfare and a professional army – a change that, in a sense, constituted the first stage in the metamorphosis of 1940.

With his return to Paris (and to a post that gave him privileged insights into the thinking of the military establishment) de Gaulle's objections to France's prevailing military strategy crystallized. The problem with the strategy was that it was exclusively defensive. On the assumption that the Great War had demonstrated the invincibility of a well-situated and thoroughly prepared defensive position, the French army had given up any thought of taking the offensive against Germany. This was unacceptable to de Gaulle on at least three grounds. First, it rested on doctrinaire assumptions about what the next war would be like. Second, it made nonsense of France's diplomatic strategy, which was based in part on a system of alliances with the smaller nations of Eastern Europe and therefore required that France be able to assist those nations militarily. Third,

6

it did not take into account recent developments in motorized warfare. De Gaulle himself had little firsthand experience of tanks, but like a number of younger officers in France and elsewhere he had long been alert to the potential of this new technology. De Gaulle did not invent, and did not claim to have invented, the principles of tank warfare or Blitzkrieg, but what he did in his third book *Vers l'armée de métier* (*Towards the Professional Army*) was to present a rhetorically powerful case for introducing these innovations into the French army.

It is sometimes suggested (and was suggested implicitly by the General himself)[12] that he would have preferred to keep his disagreement about French strategy inside the 'family' and only opted to 'politicize' his argument when it became clear that the military leadership would not listen. Although this is a natural rationalization for Gaullists uncomfortable with de Gaulle's political side, the evidence suggests that in 1933–34 de Gaulle made a conscious decision to enter the public arena. Indications of this are unmistakeable: the fact that he published the first sketch of his ideas in the *Revue politique et parlementaire* rather than in a military review; the fact that his name appeared on the frontispiece of *Vers l'armée de métier* as 'Charles de Gaulle' without indication of rank; above all, the title and form of the book itself. As many have noted, the title was provocative: 'professional army' was an expression which raised the hackles of left-of-centre republicans who had traditionally favoured a popular army and feared that a professionalized 'praetorian guard' might threaten the security of the republic. It would have been far more politic to use the bland title of the English translation: *The Army of the Future*. Nor would this have distorted the content of the book, which had more to say about the rationale for motorized armoured divisions than about the rationale for professionalizing them. The usual explanation for this 'mistake' is to attribute it to de Gaulle's taste for challenging superiors,[13] which was undoubtedly strong. But here the temperamental explanation alone misses the mark: de Gaulle acted as he did precisely because he needed to politicize the debate. If his book had simply argued for the creation of six armoured divisions, its impact could easily have been confined within the service. By tying the issue of the armoured divisions to a fundamental reform in the structure of the armed services, de Gaulle was quite deliberately removing the argument from the purely military realm and placing it in the political and parliamentary realm, where he wanted it.

Once the book had been published (to a generally warm press reception but very anaemic sales), de Gaulle immediately signalled his determination to bring its message to the attention of parliament and public. He formed alliances with a number of journalists, to whom he fed material, and at the same time cast around for parliamentarians who might be willing to promote his ideas. His published letters confirm the impression of associates such as Jean Auburtin and Gaston Palewski, who have reported de Gaulle's tenacious and single-minded pursuit of parliamentary backers.[14] Those that the Lieutenant-Colonel found were an eclectic group – and deliberately so. There were men on the left such as the socialist Léo Lagrange and the Christian democrat Philippe Serre, elder statesmen like former President of the Republic Alexandre Millerand, conservatives like Le Cour Grandmaison. The two men in whom he placed the highest hopes were the neo-socialist (and future wartime fascist) Marcel Déat and the maverick conservative Paul Reynaud. De Gaulle was introduced to Reynaud in December 1934 and the latter quickly became the chief spokesman for his ideas. At the time Reynaud was an able and rising politician, with a reputation for independence and a penchant for unpopular causes. When de Gaulle met him, he was in the midst of another unpopular but farsighted crusade, in favour of devaluing the franc. The parallels between these two anti-consensus causes were obvious. Over the next five and a half years de Gaulle kept up a close partnership with Reynaud, cajoling him to raise the issue of military reform whenever possible, coaching him about what to say, and reassuring him that high office lay in store.

This courting of politicians and journalists was a new departure for de Gaulle and a considerable risk in professional terms. It made him exceedingly unpopular with his superior officers, who were scandalized by his recourse to politics (as though literature was not bad enough!). He also made himself unpopular with many politicians – those like the Radical Party leader Daladier who were committed to the existing defence strategy as well as those on the left who had an instinctive aversion for professional soldiers. If the socialists had been privy to de Gaulle's correspondence with Reynaud, their suspicions would only have been confirmed. In June 1935 de Gaulle suggested that his professional army might have a police function at home as well as a purely military role.[15]

Association with mavericks like Reynaud and Déat was a gamble, even if de Gaulle stayed in the background and allowed his political supporters the spotlight. What prompted him to step outside the military role to which he had hitherto confined himself? It is difficult to believe that he had a sudden revelation about his superiors' inadequacy: the conservatism of the General Staff was something that he had long taken for granted. It may be that his posting to an institution at the very centre of defence planning quickened his sense of urgency. Probably more important than his new job was his participation in an informal think-tank, which was organized by a retired officer named Emile Mayer. Mayer's career in the army had been brilliant but controversial – far more controversial than de Gaulle's. Mayer had long been interested in the impact that the new technology of aircraft and tanks would have on warfare. He was an important stimulus and sounding-board for de Gaulle in 1933–34, as were the other original minds that Mayer attracted. For all that, the single event that did most to precipitate de Gaulle's 'politicization' was the coming to power of Adolf Hitler and the Nazi party. With Hitler's advent, the threat that Germany once again presented to France became an immediate one in de Gaulle's eyes. From 1933 onwards de Gaulle seems never to have doubted that Hitler's regime meant a new war between France and Germany. The insistence with which he lobbied politicians reflected his certainty about this outcome. Behind his public campaign for a professional army there was, thus, a strong sense of compulsion.

In many respects the General de Gaulle of 1940 is recognizable in the Lieutenant-Colonel de Gaulle of 1935 or 1936, although this is obscured by the subordinate role that he adopted in his relationship with Reynaud. The obsequiousness of his correspondence with Reynaud is somewhat embarrassing to Gaullists. Did he really believe, as he wrote in August 1936, that 'the day is not far off when the country will have to turn to you'?[16] Since he repeated the same prediction to third parties, he may indeed have believed it.[17] Perhaps he was also projecting his ambitions for himself onto Reynaud, just as many believe that, in the 1927 lectures on leadership, he had been thinking of himself while appearing to talk about Pétain. In any case de Gaulle was always realist enough to know when he depended on another person to achieve his ends and pragmatic enough to flatter that person's vanity: such had been the case with Pétain in the mid-1920s and was to be the case with Churchill in the early stages of Free France.

By 1937, however, it was becoming evident that his campaign had stalled. The Popular Front government that had come to office in 1936 showed no more interest in de Gaulle's ideas than its right-of-centre predecessors. Meanwhile the General Staff had closed ranks against him, almost but not quite blocking his promotion to colonel. In mid-1937 he left his post in Paris and took command of the 507th Tank Regiment in Metz. He continued to correspond with Reynaud and his supporters in Paris, but until Reynaud achieved the premiership or Daladier could be prised out of the Ministry of Defence, there was little more that de Gaulle could do. He therefore returned to his military vocation and got his first taste of commanding tanks as opposed to writing about them. In September 1939, when war broke out, he was transferred to command the tanks of the Fifth Army.

It did not take him long to realize that the German strategy would be to leave France to 'stew in her own juice'[18] for a while, and this lull (the so-called 'Phoney War') gave him one final opportunity to make his case to the General Staff and to appeal over their heads to the politicians in parliament. In January 1940 he distributed a memorandum to eighty civilian and military leaders. This memorandum reiterated the principles of *Vers l'armée de métier*, while amending their application to take into account the lessons of Germany's recent invasion of Poland (in particular, the importance of air power, which had been mentioned but not emphasized in his book). As Jean Lacouture has said, to denounce the General Staff's strategy in time of war was an audacious act, amounting to insubordination, if not outright rebellion.[19] But, for all his presumption, it is important to note that he was still playing the role of adviser. This remained so even after Reynaud finally succeeded Daladier as prime minister in March 1940. Reynaud made an effort to bring de Gaulle into the government, by appointing him Secretary of the War Cabinet, but Daladier, who retained the defence portfolio, blocked the move. So, on the eve of the German invasion, de Gaulle remained Reynaud's faithful second: 'Let us repeat that the military . . . will not reform itself by itself. It is an affair of State . . . It requires a statesman . . . You alone . . . can and must see this task to completion.' (3 May 1940)[20]

Exactly one week later the great cataclysm occurred. When German armies swept into Belgium and Northern France, de Gaulle took command of a hastily formed armoured division. His division fought two major battles with the Germans during the second half of May. As the crisis deepened, the man of character described in *The Edge of the Sword* emerged. A month after he had written the still deferential letter cited above and two days after being promoted to the rank of brigadier-general, he wrote again to Reynaud. It is not certain that Reynaud ever received the letter, but it hardly matters. The important thing is what it said about its author. De Gaulle began by stating flatly that the initial defeat resulted from Germany's application of precisely the same tactics that he had been urging on the French high command for years. Arguing that the country would welcome the emergence of 'a new man, the man for the new war', he virtually demanded that Reynaud make him Under-Secretary of State or, failing that, 'at least put me in command – not just of one of your four Armoured Divisions – but of the Armoured Corps grouping all these forces'.[21] The imperious tone of de Gaulle's missive suggested that the metamorphosis into the man of 18 June had already occurred.

.   .   .

The onset of the German offensive marked the beginning of two months of extreme turmoil for the French people. Neither their army's ninety-four divisions nor their vast and costly concrete defences (the so-called Maginot Line) nor their British allies proved able to defend them. As the enemy descended on northern and central areas of the country, ten million civilians, mostly women and children, took to the roads and headed south. On 10 June, four days before the German army reached Paris, the government itself fled the capital. On 22 June, with Pétain now in charge, the government signed an armistice with Hitler, which brought the fighting to an end but at a heavy price. The armistice divided France in two: a small southern zone was left under the control of Pétain's government, which soon established itself in the spa town of Vichy; a larger northern zone, including two-thirds of the population and much more than two-thirds of the industrial base, was placed under German control. Shortly afterwards, the republican regime which had taken France into the war effectively committed suicide by granting Pétain full powers to draw up a new constitution and to rule France in the interim.

The responses of French citizens to these disorienting events naturally varied. In some people the defeat induced apathy or a withdrawal into personal realms. Others immersed themselves in the consoling cult of Marshal Pétain. From the moment of the disaster, a few, both inside and outside France, refused to recognize the reality of defeat or the validity of the armistice that Pétain's government signed. Resistance began as individual acts of conscience, performed out of a sense of moral compulsion rather than with any practical end in sight. In one sense, de Gaulle's radio appeal falls into this category of spontaneous, almost instinctual, resistance. But de Gaulle himself saw it as something more. He was not just a dissident, nor just the leader of a group of dissidents. From the moment that he arrived in London he set out to acquire a symbolic status, not only by being the most vocal French critic of the armistice but by identifying his movement and his person with France. When one of the first people to rally to his side (a scrupulous jurist named René Cassin) inquired as to the precise legal status of Free France, de Gaulle replied: 'Nous sommes la France.'[22] In de Gaulle's conception, Free France was the only true and legitimate representative of French interests and sovereignty. He believed from the outset that Pétain's decision to sign an armistice rendered the Vichy regime illegitimate. Though he was wary about saying so in public in the early days, he also meant that he had become the personification of France. In a famous passage of his memoirs, he reconstructed his motives in June 1940: 'Faced by the frightening void of the general renunciation, my mission seemed to me, all of a sudden, clear and terrible. At this moment, the worst in her history, it was up to me to assume France.'[23] The mixture of military and religious language here is revealing. De Gaulle's call to arms can aptly be seen in both terms. A soldier's duty is to fight the enemy, and in a sense de Gaulle was doing no more than his duty in continuing the fight from England. But there was also a mystical dimension. De Gaulle sensed an intangible communion between himself and the French nation.

The reality of de Gaulle's situation in June 1940 was, in contrast, very bleak. There was an almost absurd disproportion between de Gaulle's ambitions and his means. The *appel* of 18 June rallied only a few thousand servicemen, some of whom subsequently decided to return to France. His recruitment difficulties, if anything, increased in early July, when the British navy attacked a French fleet at Mers-el-Kebir to prevent it from falling into German hands and, in so doing, touched off an explosion of French anglophobia. By the end of July there were around 7,000 men serving in Free France forces and a mere handful of senior officers. Financially and materially, de Gaulle was wholly reliant on the British government. Politically, he depended on the personal support of Winston Churchill, without whom he would not even have been able to gain access to the BBC.[24] The sentimental rapport between the two leaders deteriorated markedly as the war wore on, but in 1940 it was just strong enough to sustain de Gaulle in the early and most vulnerable stages of his enterprise. On the other hand, de Gaulle was well aware that he was not the British government's first choice to lead the Free French movement. In June 1940 the British made several attempts to lure a bigger name (a more senior politician like Reynaud or a higher-ranking general like Weygand) to London. It was only when these attempts failed that the British government recognized de Gaulle as 'leader of all Free Frenchmen' (28 June).

What did it mean, though, to be leader of all Free

Frenchmen? At a moment when Britain was preparing to face the coming German onslaught and a government in France was cooperating with the German occupation forces, the concept seemed to have purely symbolic significance. To many people it seemed no more real than the project for Anglo-French unification which Jean Monnet, de Gaulle, and Churchill had concocted in mid-June in a desperate attempt to stiffen the Reynaud government's resistance. Far from being swept into power like the man of character in *The Edge of the Sword,* de Gaulle was a largely unrecognized and marginal figure. To fulfil his claim to have 'assumed' France, he faced daunting obstacles: the minuscule dimensions of his own movement, which could fit at first into a single building; the veneration in which his rival, Marshal Pétain, was held by the mass of the French people and the diplomatic recognition that Vichy received from the US, USSR, and many other nations; and, within a matter of months, the disenchantment and open hostility of his own allies. It would be difficult to imagine a more inauspicious beginning for the greatest political career in twentieth-century French history.

. . .

NOTES AND REFERENCES

1. Malraux A 1971 *Les Chênes qu'on abat.* Gallimard, Paris, p. 107.
2. De Gaulle C 1954 *Mémoires de guerre* (3 vols). Plon, Paris, vol. 1 pp. 267–8.
3. De Gaulle C 1954 vol. 1 p. 71.
4. Barrès P 1941 *Charles de Gaulle.* Hachette, Edinburgh, pp. 14, 19.
5. Lacouture J 1984 *De Gaulle* (3 vols). Le Seuil, Paris, vol. 1 p. 427.
6. Pouget J 1973 *Un certain capitaine de Gaulle.* Fayard, Paris, p. 11.
7. Cassin R 1975 *Les Hommes partis de rien.* Plon, Paris, pp. 122–3.
8. LNC vol. 1 pp. 7–23.
9. Tournoux J-R 1966 *Pétain and de Gaulle* trans O Coburn. Viking, New York, pp. 50–1.
10. Tournoux J-R 1966 pp. 46–8. This anecdote is recounted in numerous other biographies.
11. LNC vol. 2 pp. 331–3.

12. De Gaulle C 1954 vol. 1 p. 11.
13. Lacouture J 1984 vol. 1 p. 236.
14. Auburtin J 1965 *Le Colonel de Gaulle.* Plon, Paris, p. 144; Lacouture J 1984 vol. 1 pp. 244–5.
15. LNC vol. 2 p. 393.
16. LNC vol. 2 p. 409.
17. Letter to Col. Mayer, LNC vol. 12 p. 261.
18. LNC vol. 2 p. 486; LNC vol. 12 p. 271.
19. Lacouture J 1984 vol. 1 pp. 300–01.
20. LNC vol. 2 p. 493.
21. Letter of 3/6/40, LNC vol. 3 pp. 476–7.
22. Cassin R 1975 p. 77.
23. De Gaulle C 1954 vol. 1 p. 74.
24. Kersaudy F 1982 *Churchill and de Gaulle.* Collins and Atheneum, New York, pp. 77–8.

Chapter 2

1940–44: SYMBOL

De Gaulle's years of wartime exile (1940–44) divide naturally into two periods. The first was the heroic period in London between June 1940 and May 1943. In this founding era, de Gaulle gradually gathered soldiers and civilians to his standard, transformed his improvised organization into an alternative state, with its own bureaucracy and armed forces, headed off efforts to replace him as Free France's leader, and emerged as the symbolic head of all French resisters, inside as well as outside France. These years saw a shift in both French and foreign perceptions of legitimacy away from Vichy and in favour of de Gaulle and Free France.

Then, at the end of May 1943, de Gaulle left England and flew to French Algeria, which had been liberated by the Americans six months earlier. There he presided over the expansion of his French National Committee into a new, more broadly based provisional government known as the French Committee of National Liberation (CFLN – Comité Français de Libération Nationale). In the year that followed his arrival in Algeria, the focus of his activity shifted. The challenge now was to prepare for the transfer of his state and his army back to France. The London period had been primarily a test of willpower and improvisation. The challenges of the North African year were primarily those of planning and organization.

At the beginning, priorities had been dictated by his scarce resources. To keep France in the war against Germany, de Gaulle needed to recruit French servicemen and civilians. That made it essential to continue making contact with France via regular radio broadcasts and to forge links with French communities abroad. But the largest readily accessible reservoir of support lay in the French empire, which the Germans did not occupy and where Vichy's authority was uncertain. From the outset, therefore, the empire was central to de Gaulle's strategy. It was no coincidence that the first official title of the Free French movement's executive – a title which de Gaulle had suggested to Churchill as early as July 1940 – was the *Conseil de Défense de l'Empire*.[1] In de Gaulle's mind, the empire was more than just a source of potential recruits. Any territories that rallied to Free France would enhance the legitimacy of his movement, provide strategic bases for his forces, and perhaps even give him the opportunity to transfer his headquarters to a base on French soil. Above all, the empire was the only place where he could make good immediately on his claim to represent the real France.[2]

At first this strategy produced disappointing results, as the French authorities in North Africa, Indochina, and Syria rallied to Vichy. However, there were also some modest but significant successes. In June and July, a number of small French outposts in the Indian and Pacific Oceans responded to his appeal. On 26 August, the territory of Chad in French Equatorial Africa and its governor Félix Eboué rallied to Free France. On 27 August Cameroon followed suit, and Congo did so one day later. These successes encouraged de Gaulle to press ahead with a more ambitious operation, which he had proposed to Churchill a month earlier. His plan was to launch a Free French expedition, supported by British warships, to rally the important port city of Dakar, the capital of French West Africa. With Churchill's prodding, the British Chiefs-of-Staff had agreed to participate in the operation, albeit in modified form, and on 31 August an Anglo-Free French expedition set out from Liverpool. From the beginning, however, the operation was dogged by mistakes and misfortunes. These culminated on 23–24 September, when the pro-Vichy forces in Dakar vigorously resisted a Free French landing, and de Gaulle and his forces were compelled to withdraw.

The Dakar fiasco came close to ending de Gaulle's political career almost before it had begun. Wherever responsibility for the mistakes lay – and it lay with Churchill

17

and the British as much as with the Free French – the failure was a colossal humiliation for de Gaulle, because it showed an imperial administration utterly loyal to Vichy and more than capable of repelling the Free French. In the short term, de Gaulle was carried through the crisis by the personal support of Churchill (who defended him before the House of Commons) and by his own reserves of self-assurance. To fight off a deep depression, he concentrated his thoughts on the larger picture, telling his wife at the end of September that 'the "Battle of Britain" is now won . . . American intervention seems to me certain'.[3]

The prospects for his movement, however, were not so rosy. Dakar proved to be the last occasion that de Gaulle's efforts to win over territories in the empire were conducted in close and sincere collaboration with his allies. The lessons that the British and later the Americans drew from Dakar were twofold: first, the operational and political disadvantages of collaborative expeditions with Free France; and second, the practical necessity of working with or at least through Vichy's imperial administrators. This concession to Vichy was unacceptable to de Gaulle on grounds of self-interest, because it reduced the stature and role of Free France. It was also, in his view, unpardonable on grounds of principle, since by the autumn of 1940 Vichy seemed to be aligning itself with the foreign policy of the Nazi regime and with aspects of its political ideology.

The issue of the empire contributed to the growing tenseness of de Gaulle's relations with his allies, but it did not create the rift, the fundamental cause of which was the General's interpretation of his own mission. When he said to Cassin 'Nous sommes la France', he did not mean it in a rhetorical sense. The Allies (certainly the British) would have been perfectly happy for de Gaulle to claim a generalized legitimacy on the grounds that he represented the true interests of France. But de Gaulle understood the claim in a literal sense: in his view Free France *was* France, and he was the head of a sovereign French government. Other factors – such as de Gaulle's deep-rooted suspicion of British designs on the French empire and the personal animosities which developed between him and various British and American officials – aggravated tensions but their root cause was a complete disagreement as to whether Free

France should act and be treated as an independent sovereign power.

This divergence began to emerge at a very early stage. The first real signs of trouble appeared in January 1941, when British Intelligence wrongly accused a prominent Free French official, Vice-Admiral Muselier, of spying for Vichy. De Gaulle reacted sharply, not just because the evidence against Muselier appeared flimsy, but because he interpreted the British action as an attempt to interfere in the internal affairs of his organization.

The Muselier affair provided a mere foretaste of what was to follow. Over the next eighteen months, de Gaulle's relations with the British government deteriorated dramatically. The most serious breach occurred in the spring and summer of 1941 as a result of a crisis in the Middle East. The problems there began when de Gaulle flew out to Cairo in the hope of launching an expedition to rally the French mandated territories of Syria and Lebanon. The initial response of British officials in the region was wary. Mindful of recent events in Dakar, these officials believed that Allied interests would best be served by maintaining a working relationship with Vichy administrators. They were soon forced to reverse their opinion, however, when Vichy allowed German planes to land in Syria. Grudgingly the British now agreed to a joint expedition, but they were determined to launch it on their own terms, which were quite different from de Gaulle's. The British regarded it as essential to win over Arab opinion by promising postwar independence for Syria and Lebanon; de Gaulle regarded this as British colonialist meddling in French affairs, and when the British tried to issue a declaration promising independence in their own name as well as Free France's, he objected that the future of French mandates was none of Britain's business. Anglo-Gaullist disagreements intensified once the expedition got under way.[4] The British pointedly refused to endorse the two major conditions that de Gaulle placed on an armistice with the local authorities: an opportunity for Free France to administer the mandated territories and recruit soldiers and civilians from them; and a guarantee that the British would respect all of France's rights in the region. When he realized that he was unlikely to receive satisfaction on either score, de Gaulle distanced himself from the negotiations by flying to Brazzaville in Central Africa. In the end, the crisis reached a partial resolution. After the British had signed an armistice with the Vichy administration, a number of Gaullist 'explosions' (the most celebrated of which was a stormy interview between de Gaulle and the British minister of state in Cairo, Oliver Lyttelton) forced a modification of the armistice terms so as to accommodate the General's objections. But it was not a happy resolution for either party. Churchill had been alienated by de Gaulle's harsh attacks on British policy and British officials. De Gaulle had been exasperated by what he interpreted as British perfidy. And in spite of the compromise, five-sixths of the 30,000 Vichy troops in Syria and Lebanon were permitted to return to France and thereby lost to Free France.

When de Gaulle returned to London at the end of August 1941, he and Churchill had a making-up of sorts, but behind the scenes British officials were now working to replace de Gaulle as head of the movement. On two occasions, in September 1941 and again in early 1942, they prompted Admiral Muselier to attempt a palace revolution against de Gaulle.[5] Both attempts failed. Then, in May 1942, there was a re-run of the Middle East crisis, this time over Madagascar. Again, de Gaulle had approached the British government with a proposal for a Free French expedition to rally a strategically important part of the French empire. Again the British at first dragged their feet, but eventually decided to launch an operation, this time without any Free French participation whatsoever. Once the operation had begun, the pattern of the Middle East crisis was repeated. The British initially negotiated with the Vichy authorities and showed no enthusiasm for replacing them with Free French officials, and in the end made belated concessions to appease Free French sensibilities.

When de Gaulle challenged Churchill about Madagascar, the prime minister reminded the General that he was not Britain's only ally.[6] De Gaulle interpreted this to mean that Churchill had excluded Free French forces in order to please his American allies. True or not, it was a fact that, by this stage of the war, six months after Pearl Harbor, de Gaulle had to confront American leadership in the alliance. The hostility he encountered from Washington was far more deep-rooted and systematic than anything he had experienced in London. Franklin Roosevelt had maintained a diplomatic representative in Vichy from the outset. Unlike the sentimental francophile in Downing Street, the American president believed that France had ceased, for the foreseeable future, to be a great power. He did not expect the French empire to be reconstituted at the end of the war. He was also utterly allergic to the suggestion that de Gaulle or anybody else could have legitimacy until the French people had expressed their preferences in democratic fashion. The Americans viewed de Gaulle's assumption of France as the delusion of an egotist with fascistic tendencies.

Given the preponderant influence of the US within the anti-Axis alliance, this hostility posed a very serious threat to de Gaulle. Yet, while many of his followers fretted about it, de Gaulle viewed the situation with remarkable sangfroid. Again, he took consolation in the larger picture. His perspective was that in 1942 – unlike in 1940 – his movement no longer depended exclusively on the support of its allies or on its capacity to rally French overseas territories. The key now was the growing resistance to Vichy and the Nazis inside France and the identification of this resistance with Gaullism. In May 1942, he told his senior officials: 'We have now established many contacts with metropolitan France, all of which prove that the nation is really gathering around our standard . . . Our allies are aware of this state of opinion in France. They note it often with bad grace . . . But they have to take it as a fact, and it is a fact which prevents them from envisaging our liquidation.'[7] The events of November 1942–June 1943 were to confirm this analysis.

Operation Torch – the American invasion of French North Africa in November 1942 – was the culmination of Allied attempts to exclude de Gaulle and to promote a viable alternative to Gaullism. When Roosevelt had been persuaded by the British, in July 1942, to postpone a direct invasion of Western Europe and instead to prepare an invasion of North Africa, one of his conditions had been that Free France should be excluded. But American aims went beyond the mere exclusion of Free France from this particular theatre of operations. Once they had landed in

North Africa, the Americans hoped to establish an anti-Gaullist, pro-Allied French movement there, to be headed by a prominent military figure. The prime candidate for the job was General Henri Giraud, a courageous soldier who had opposed the armistice in 1940 and had been imprisoned by the Germans before escaping early in 1942. From the American perspective, Giraud had the twin advantages of outranking de Gaulle and of being totally uninterested in politics (he later proved incompetent as well as uninterested). There was also some talk that Admiral François Darlan, Pétain's prime minister in 1941 and early 1942, might be persuaded to head an anti-German movement in North Africa.

De Gaulle had got wind of the Allied invasion plan in August 1942, but he was probably unaware of its full political implications. Ignorance, combined with confidence that the popular support that he enjoyed inside France would make him indispensable to the Allies, may well explain his initially calm response to news of the invasion on 8 November.[8] His radio broadcast on the same day contained no hint of criticism of the Allies. At that point, de Gaulle assumed that Giraud would play a purely military role in the operation and he had no inkling that Darlan would become involved in it. Over the following days, the picture changed radically – and with it de Gaulle's attitude.

In advance of the operation, the Americans had assumed that Giraud's prestige in French North Africa would clear the way to a rapid ceasefire. In fact, however, Giraud arrived on the scene two days later than planned and, when he did arrive, proved less influential than anticipated. Faced by unexpectedly heavy resistance, the American commanders transferred their attention to Admiral Darlan, who in mysterious circumstances had flown to Algiers shortly before the invasion. On 10 November the American General Clark signed an armistice with Darlan. Three days later Darlan was recognized by the US as High Commissioner for North Africa. He was assisted by an Imperial Council consisting of Giraud and four Vichy-appointed officials. This compromise with Vichy in the interests of a quick military success was too blatant for de Gaulle (or indeed for many British and American officials) to stomach. At the same time, it presented him with colossal political opportunities. In Britain and the US, the cynicism of the 'Darlan deal' immediately cast de Gaulle in the role of principled critic. By publicly opposing the recourse to a notorious Vichyite, he could also crystallize pro-Gaullist feeling within the French Resistance. It is true that his criticisms further antagonized the American administration, but de Gaulle willingly took the gamble, believing that his survival now depended more on the French people than on Roosevelt.

De Gaulle's lucidity on this point was eventually justified by events, but not before the Americans had made a concerted effort to eliminate him as a political force. When Darlan was assassinated, on Christmas Eve 1942, the Americans put pressure on the Imperial Council to appoint their man, Giraud, as his successor. On 26 December Giraud took office as Civil and Military Commander-in-Chief. The following month, meeting at Casablanca, Roosevelt and Churchill tried to coerce de Gaulle into merging Free France with Giraud's organization. De Gaulle himself had proposed a merger in December (and received a good press in the US and Britain for having done so).[9] But his idea of a merger was quite different from the Allied proposal, which would have ruled out the possibility of a provisional French government and subordinated de Gaulle to Giraud. De Gaulle held his ground and, not for the first time, even contemplated a break with the Allies rather than accept their demands.[10]

Roosevelt then tried a more subtle approach. In February 1943 he despatched Jean Monnet to Algiers to act as his personal envoy to Giraud.[11] Monnet's mission was twofold: to improve Giraud's reactionary image in the Allied press by eliminating the most blatant traces of Vichy rule in North Africa; and to find a formula for unifying Giraudists and Gaullists in such a way as to absorb de Gaulle's movement into a larger and less political organization. De Gaulle's response to this initiative was a calculated mixture of flexibility and intransigence. He welcomed every liberal concession that Monnet wrung out of Giraud, who was fundamentally a reactionary. He agreed to send a representative, General Catroux, to negotiate with the Giraudists. But he remained unshakeable on two critical issues: first, that Giraud should not be the sole head of the unified movement; and second, that the movement should be a true provisional government, not an administrative caretaker.

Throughout the spring of 1943 the British and Americans tried to force de Gaulle into accepting what they presented as a reasonable compromise on these issues. Indeed de Gaulle's own negotiator advised the General to accept a compromise. But de Gaulle held firm because he knew that time was working in his favour. Pro-Gaullist sentiment was building in North Africa, while inside France de Gaulle's agent, Jean Moulin, was negotiating the unification of the resistance movements under Gaullist patronage.

In the end, as he had anticipated, events inside France proved critical. On 15 May 1943 representatives of the major resistance movements met in Paris to form a National Council of the Resistance (CNR – Conseil National de la Résistance), which immediately declared that 'the people of France will never accept the subordination of General de Gaulle to General Giraud' and demanded 'the rapid installation of a provisional government in Algiers under the presidency of General de Gaulle, with General Giraud as military chief'. Confronted by this statement, Giraud accepted de Gaulle's demand for a central French authority to be headed jointly by the two men. On 30 May de Gaulle landed at an airstrip at Boufarik outside Algiers. He had engineered a unification of all French forces opposed to Vichy and to the Axis powers on his own terms and, soon, under his sole leadership.

. . .

In view of the inauspiciousness of the beginnings, de Gaulle's successes between June 1940 and May 1943 were indeed remarkable. How had he managed to confirm his own legitimacy, reduce the legitimacy of Vichy, resist Allied attempts to marginalize him, and gain the recognition of the resistance movements?

At the risk of stating the obvious, one might say that de Gaulle won his quarrel with Pétain because he correctly predicted the course of the war and Pétain did not. The assumption of the Vichy regime in signing the armistice with Hitler had been that the war, to all intents and purposes, was over. Britain would either be overwhelmed as

France had been or would seek a compromise with Hitler. De Gaulle's assumption in June 1940 was precisely the opposite: that Britain would survive and that sooner or later Germany would be defeated. He presented this assumption not so much as a prediction as a factual observation: 'This war has not been settled by the battle of France. This war is a world war.' (18 June 1940)

At every stage of the ensuing conflict de Gaulle was able to stay ahead of events. By September 1940 he was taking British survival for granted and predicting American intervention. He also foresaw the likelihood of a war between Germany and the Soviet Union.[12] From the moment that both future superpowers entered the war, he regarded Allied victory as inevitable.

His prescience gave de Gaulle a moral advantage over Vichy as well as a symbolic seniority among resisters. Having raised his standard at the very nadir of France's fortunes, when to do so seemed a hopeless and almost irrational gesture, he claimed the high ground of principle for himself. Everybody who came to resistance after 18 June 1940 was, to some degree, forced to look up to de Gaulle. Furthermore inside his organization his prescience produced bonds of intense devotion and trust. The recollections of those who worked with him in the war years show a striking convergence:[13] volunteers were won over instantly by the self-assured prophetic tone in which he discussed the war and by his knack of making them feel that they had been singled out to receive a confidence.

Of course, the moral or symbolic stature that he gained from making the right choice at the outset did not guarantee de Gaulle his triumphant arrival in North Africa in mid-1943. To exploit his stature, de Gaulle had to create an organization from scratch, fend off rivals to his legitimacy, and dodge the attempts of his 'allies' (he used quotation marks on occasion) to remove him. He achieved success through the combination of a vigilant, resourceful, and tough 'inside game' with the skilful projection of his image and view of events.

Inside his own organization de Gaulle attached immediate priority to creating a centralized power structure. He insisted that he alone set Free French policy on all major issues. He decided on all military promotions and made the important non-military appointments. He was adamant that all dealings with Allied governments – even those transacted at distant points in the French Empire – should be referred to him. Occasionally in the early months his subordinates deliberately or accidentally transgressed these rules and promptly had their knuckles rapped. Over time, as the movement expanded and bureaucratized, he was forced to relax his personal supervision. However, he always retained control over the issues that he regarded as most important (which is not to say that they were necessarily the most important in an objective sense). Furthermore, by broadening his own identity from leader of the London dissidents to leader of the whole French Resistance, internal as well as external, he remained, in a sense, bigger than his own organization.

This autocratic structure, combined with the military style in which he managed it, aroused the hostility of some members of the Free French community, as well as members of the British and American governments. It provoked charges of authoritarianism and encouraged attempts to replace him. However, it also made it very difficult for dissidence to succeed. Nobody inside the movement was permitted to acquire enough power or a high enough profile to challenge de Gaulle successfully. When somebody tried to do so, he was treated not like a party politician challenging his leader but like a soldier threatening to desert. There was an element of incongruity with his own behaviour, of course: de Gaulle had himself deserted in 1940, and had been tried and sentenced by Vichy *in absentia.* But de Gaulle never felt compelled to recognize the military hierarchy which existed before 18 June 1940 except when it suited his interests to do so.

In meeting challenges to his authority, de Gaulle's tactics were simple, but effective. He was utterly intransigent on what he defined as essential principles: the hierarchy within Free France, French sovereignty over areas belonging to France in 1939, and his personal legitimacy. Rather than compromise on these principles, he preferred to withdraw from the scene and wait out his opponents. He also resorted, on occasion, to resignation threats and to attempts to play one ally off against another (for example by developing a close relationship with the Soviet government).

These high-handed tactics were obviously risky, but they were a calculated risk. In terms of power relations, the odds were stacked against him. De Gaulle could only survive by continually raising the stakes over issues that were crucial to his position but not so crucial to the British or Americans.

The other way in which he could compensate for unfavourable power relations was through effective public relations. Like many people on both sides of the conflict, de Gaulle recognized that the Second World War was a war which had to be waged with words and images as well as guns and bombs. In his case words and the mental images that they created were the only available means of communication with his people. Since he had not been a public figure before the war, the mass of French people had no idea what he looked like. Nor did they have any preconceptions about his personality or politics. To a degree this made him vulnerable: Vichy propagandists had an opportunity to fill in the blanks, by vilifying him as a deserter in the pay of the British or of Jewish interests. But in the end it proved an enormous advantage. First, it was easier for a disembodied voice like de Gaulle to 'assume' France than it would have been for a more recognizable figure, about whom people had already formed settled views. Second, de Gaulle proved exceptionally well-suited to this role of disembodied voice. In his sixty-seven wartime broadcasts over the BBC he displayed, for the first time, his formidable communication skills. His measured, serene commentary on the progress of the war inspired confidence. The flashes of ridicule or condescension that he directed at the 'old men' in Vichy undermined confidence in his opponents. Above all, his direct, intimate, but emotionally charged style gave listeners huddled around their receivers in occupied France the sense that he was talking to each of them. At first the numbers of those who tuned in to the BBC were modest in comparison to those who listened to Pétain's homilies on Radio Vichy. But over time his audience grew, and in part at least this was a tribute to his success as a radio voice.[14]

De Gaulle always regarded this audience inside France as his main one. To convert the assumed legitimacy of 1940 into actual legitimacy, de Gaulle needed the support of the

French people. That was his absolute priority. In 1940 and 1941, for example, it would have done his image in America an enormous amount of good if he had wrapped himself in the mantle of French democracy. Nevertheless, at the risk of confirming suspicions that he was a political reactionary, he scrupulously avoided discussion of internal French politics (except to criticize Vichy for collaborating with the Germans). He was wary of identifying himself to the French people as a 'democrat' at a time when democracy was equated with the detested Third Republic.[15] In 1942 and 1943, he gradually broke this silence, but not to appease Roosevelt. His new democratic commitment emerged as a response to the republicanism of the resistance movements inside France.

That said, he also appreciated the importance of influencing public opinion outside France, particularly in Britain and the US. In his memoirs he reconstructed his reasoning thus: 'while . . . the great men carried Anglo-Saxon public opinion along with them, public opinion, in its turn, in spite of wartime censorship, guided the governments.'[16] In other words, his strategy was to gain leverage over his powerful patrons by manipulating their own publics against them. His resolute and solitary stand against the armistice established a favourable impression at the outset, and he worked effectively to preserve this initial impression. He could rely on some influential supporters in both the British and the American presses. He was also not above an occasional public relations ploy. In early 1942, for example, he allowed himself to be photographed with Madame de Gaulle in a domestic 'off-duty' setting. The shots, which were widely reprinted in the Allied press, showed a relaxed General listening to his wife play the piano or watching her knit. Their subtext was that this was a devoted husband and a decent chap, not the apprentice dictator that his detractors portrayed.[17] In general, de Gaulle's rapport with Allied publics was remarkably good, especially in view of the fact that he had no prior experience of either country, spoke at best a halting English, and had to overcome systematic attempts by the governments to influence press coverage against him. Though popularity did not necessarily translate into greater recognition in official circles, it did inhibit those in the two governments who would have liked to ditch him altogether. That was particularly true at the end of 1942, when de Gaulle was able to exploit public outrage over the Darlan deal to boost his own image and thwart plans for his replacement.

Roosevelt might nevertheless have got his way in 1943, had it not been for developments inside France. Throughout his long struggle with Giraud, de Gaulle depicted himself as the one who was in touch with the aspirations of the Resistance. This identification put Giraud and his American backers on the defensive and ultimately proved to be de Gaulle's trump card.

The manner in which he obtained and manipulated the Resistance's timely endorsement was symptomatic of his methods. In 1940 and 1941 there had been few links between Free France and the clandestine movements in France. Though resisters were often called 'Gaullists' by Vichy officials or Germans, this was largely because 'Gaullist', like 'communist', had become a broad term of abuse. It was not until 1942 that the internal and external Resistances established close and regular links. These links were made possible, in the first instance, by a few brave Gaullist agents, most notably a former prefect called Jean Moulin who returned to France in January 1942 with instructions from de Gaulle to promote the unification of resistance movements. Moulin's behind-the-scenes work would probably not have gone very far, however, without a public appeal from de Gaulle to the leaders of the Resistance. In March 1942 de Gaulle received his first visit from the leader of a clandestine movement (Christian Pineau of the movement *Libération-Nord*).[18] Pineau informed de Gaulle about the strongly republican and socialist trend of resistance ideology and tried to persuade him to abandon his political reticence, which was causing concern among resisters. It is fair to assume that not everything in the emerging resistance ideology pleased de Gaulle. The first declaration he gave to Pineau to take back to France would almost certainly have disappointed resisters: its denunciation of the Third Republic was a little too sweeping for Pineau's taste (one has to remember that by this stage the bitter experience of Vichyism and Nazism was beginning to rehabilitate the reputation of republicanism in France), and it had almost nothing to say about social or economic reform. At the last moment, however, de Gaulle's tactical sense asserted itself: he revised his message so as to emphasize his ideological opposition to Vichy, embrace the political tradition of liberty, equality, and fraternity, and acknowledge the necessity of a postwar social transformation.

This declaration, dated 23 June 1942, was published both in London and in various clandestine journals in France. It is often called the *appel à la Résistance*, which is an apt term because it implies an analogy with the speech of 18 June 1940. The first *appel* had been the declaration of a military man, calling on French soldiers to continue the fight. The second was the appeal of a politician to his constituency.

This politicization of de Gaulle's message was a critical stage in the evolution towards a unified resistance. But it would be a distortion to suggest that de Gaulle and his agents were solely responsible for the eventual unification. That would be to ignore the role of the influential Communist Party and of grass-roots pressure within the movements. It would also overlook the substantial differences of perception and priority between de Gaulle and Moulin, on the one hand, and the resistance leaders, on the other. For all the importance that de Gaulle attached to securing the support of the Resistance, he was determined to secure it on his terms, i.e. in such a way as to reinforce his leadership and legitimize his movement before world opinion. In the critical early months of 1943 he was prepared to disappoint and even antagonize resistance leaders in his pursuit of this objective. Thus, in order to increase the perceived representativeness of the National Council of the Resistance and to dilute the influence of the Communist Party within it, he insisted that all the major prewar parties – even the centrist and conservative parties which were mere phantoms in 1943 – should be represented in it alongside the resistance movements.

This decision to resurrect groups which symbolized what de Gaulle, as much as the resisters, regarded as a bankrupt political tradition caused a considerable stir. Resisters argued that it opened the way for a return to prewar politics. Certain Gaullists, especially left-wing ones like the socialist Pierre Brossolette, agreed with them. But de Gaulle's decision reflected his sense of priorities. De Gaulle saw his movement as the provisional French government, whose responsibility was the preservation of the nation's rank and reputation. Resistance unity, in his view, served a purpose only if it served the interests of his 'state'. Resisters, on the other hand, saw themselves as the nation-in-arms. Their struggle was to achieve revolution from below rather than continuity from above.

In other words, de Gaulle and the Resistance began from different points. Though their paths converged, in part because of de Gaulle's and Moulin's different but complementary skills, the convergence was transitory. It certainly did not mean that the two movements had been fused into a single whole. After Moulin's capture by the Germans in June 1943, the CNR was never again to be headed by the CFLN's representative. Moulin had bequeathed to de Gaulle undoubted precedence over the resistance leadership, but he had not bequeathed – and probably could never have bequeathed – a complete identity of outlook between internal and external resistance.

. . . .

Almost exactly a year separated de Gaulle's arrival in Algiers from the Allied landings in Normandy, which paved the way for the liberation of France. If anything, this period saw a stepping-up in the pace of his activity. There was plenty of old business still to be settled. For example, he had to finish off Giraud and establish sole command over the CFLN. He was also confronted by continuing obstruction and hostility from Roosevelt, the US State Department, and Churchill (though by this stage he could at least count on some support from the Foreign Office). At the same time, there was pressing new business: the setting up of a provisional state in North Africa, preparation for its transfer back to France, supervision of the French war effort, and planning for postwar reconstruction.

Disposing of Giraud took a relatively short time. De Gaulle engineered a majority for himself on the CFLN and promptly objected to Giraud's claim to combine the functions of Commander-in-Chief with the co-presidency. To press his case, de Gaulle again employed the tactics of withdrawal and threatened resignation that he had used with the British in 1941 and 1942.[19] At Roosevelt's behest, the

US Commander-in-Chief, General Eisenhower, tried to force de Gaulle to back down by threatening to cut off American supplies to the French army if Giraud were removed. These threats backfired: Eisenhower's ultimatum offended the members of the CFLN and encouraged them to adopt a solution that favoured de Gaulle. Over the following months, de Gaulle assumed total control over political affairs and substantially reduced Giraud's authority as Commander-in-Chief.

Giraud's political demise only intensified the frustration and annoyance of the British and American governments with de Gaulle. The next few months saw a series of incidents – some petty, some serious – which kept relations tense. In November 1943 the Middle East crisis flared up again, when the British intervened on behalf of the Lebanese government. The following month Roosevelt and Churchill tried to prevent de Gaulle from conducting legal proceedings against former Vichy officials. There was also a brief but bitter controversy surrounding British allegations of torture by Gaullist officials in London (the so-called 'Dufour Affair' to which de Gaulle devoted a full four pages in his war memoirs).

Far more serious for de Gaulle and the CFLN was the prospect of their exclusion from Allied planning for the forthcoming invasion of France. The invasion had received final approval from the 'Big Three' (Churchill, Roosevelt, and Stalin) in their meeting at Teheran in December 1943. While de Gaulle did not find it difficult to detect what was in the air, there was little that he could do to influence Allied planning directly. What he could and did do, throughout the Algiers year, was to strengthen the CFLN's position inside and outside France so that, whenever the operation began, the CFLN would be in the best position to preempt Allied attempts to marginalize it.

This preemptive action took four forms. The first involved bolstering the CFLN's claims to legitimacy, both in French eyes and in the view of foreign governments and publics. To do this, de Gaulle reshuffled his committee to include more representatives of the Resistance and more familiar political faces. He also created a Consultative Assembly in Algiers, where representatives from the Resistance sat alongside members of the Third Republic's final parliament. This assembly was a symbol of de Gaulle's commitment to republicanism. It also provided a forum in which French men and women of differing political persuasions could express their confidence in the CFLN and its president. Though he was later subtly dismissive of the assembly, he undoubtedly appreciated its value at the time, not least for the good publicity it gave him in the British and American press. He attended the assembly's sessions regularly and on several occasions used it as a parliamentary forum in which to press his case.

The second aspect of de Gaulle's preemptive strategy involved the creation of an extensive administrative network inside France. De Gaulle was aware of US plans to install in liberated areas of France an Allied Military Government of Occupied Territories (AMGOT) similar to the one in liberated Italy. To forestall that eventuality and, at the same time, ensure an orderly transition from German or Vichy administration, de Gaulle approved a series of important ordinances in the first four months of 1944. In January he created eighteen regional *Commissaires de la République*, whose function would be to supervise the post-liberation transition. His delegates in France immediately set to work to nominate these regional administrators. They also nominated reliable people to take over prefectures and senior posts in the central ministries in Paris. Later, in March and April, de Gaulle approved ordinances specifying how liberated areas were to be governed and how and when a National Assembly would be convened. Some of these decisions remained dead letters in the event, but collectively they demonstrated de Gaulle's determination that the only qualified civilian authority in liberated France would be the CFLN.

The third element in de Gaulle's strategy in 1944 was a renewed effort to maximize the CFLN's military contribution. In the early stages of the war, most of Free France's fighting, by force of circumstances, had been against other Frenchmen – in Africa, the Middle East, and elsewhere. But in mid-1942, at Bir-Hakeim in the Libyan desert, Free French forces had scored their first significant victory against German forces, and this had been followed by other successful actions in North Africa. In early 1944, de Gaulle regarded it as essential that French forces, which now numbered 400,000 men, should play a leading role in the campaigns to liberate Europe. He followed with particular attention the progress of General Juin's French Expeditionary Force, which fought alongside the Allies in Italy and in May 1944 achieved a crucial breakthrough in the German line south of Rome. De Gaulle used Juin's significant contribution in Italy as an argument in favour of French participation in the Normandy landings.

The fourth and final part of the strategy involved formulating plans for a national 'renovation' after the war.[20] This focus on reconstruction put the CFLN in step with the resistance movements and the CNR, which had been discussing postwar renewal with increasing urgency ever since the American landings in North Africa. It also conveyed the message that the CFLN – which renamed itself the Provisional Government of the French Republic (GPRF –Gouvernement Provisoire de la République Française) as of June 1944 – had a role beyond liberation. Indicative of this growing concern with postwar reconstruction was de Gaulle's trip to Brazzaville in French Equatorial Africa at the end of January 1944. The so-called Brazzaville Conference that he convened there considered various proposals for political, social, and economic reforms in French Africa. Its liberal recommendations reflected de Gaulle's own view that France had to satisfy African demands for development, not with a view to eventual decolonization, but on the contrary in order to tie the empire more securely to France in the postwar era. Both in its reformist tendencies and in its underlying conservatism, the conference set the tone for France's postwar colonial policy.

In retrospect, it is clear that this preemptive strategy succeeded: in most areas of France, the transfer of power into the hands of the Gaullist state went relatively smoothly; Vichy's bureaucracy put up no substantial resistance to de Gaulle; and the AMGOT threat was averted. However, this outcome had been by no means certain when de Gaulle flew back to England on 4 June 1944, to be briefed about the invasion which was about to begin. The American government had already printed 'French' currency, to be distributed in liberated areas, and the Allied Commander-in-Chief, General Eisenhower, had prepared a proclamation to the French people which made no mention of de Gaulle or the CFLN. De Gaulle's foul temper in the days immediately before and after the Normandy landings reflected more than just annoyance at the exclusion of his movement: he was still confident that events were moving in his favour, but the huge imponderable of American intentions remained a source of concern.[21]

De Gaulle's moroseness did not last long. On 14 June, he paid his first visit to liberated territory in Normandy. The acclaim that he encountered in the streets of two Norman towns (Isigny and Bayeux) proved a turning point. With this clear evidence of de Gaulle's popularity, the Allies gradually shelved their AMGOT plans. In early July de Gaulle paid his first visit to the US, where he received a warm welcome. At the end of the visit Roosevelt issued a statement, timed to coincide with the General's return to Algiers, recognizing the CFLN as 'qualified to carry out the administration of France'.

The major unresolved issue for the General now was the pace of the liberation and the transition to Gaullist administration. After the initial successes of the Normandy landings, the Allied armies had been pinned down by the Germans. As late as the end of July, it was conceivable that the liberation of Paris might be months away.[22] Even after the US Third Army under Patton made the crucial breakthrough on 31 July, Eisenhower had no immediate plans to liberate Paris. This delay concerned de Gaulle for two reasons. First, the liberation of the capital had, in his mind, a symbolic significance which went beyond purely military considerations. But, second, he had pressing political reasons to want a rapid liberation of Paris. The political situation in the country was dangerously fluid. De Gaulle knew that collaborators around the Vichy prime minister Pierre Laval were trying desperately to resuscitate the Third Republic as a way of saving their own skins and forestalling a Gaullist takeover. He was also concerned (according to his memoirs) that the communists would use the cover of anti-German insurrections (such as that which began in Paris in August) to launch a revolution of their own. It is very difficult to know how seriously to take these fears. The memoirs were written in a very anti-communist phase of his life, and we know that at the time he received indirect assurances from the head of the Communist Party,

Maurice Thorez, that no insurrection was being planned.[23] On the other hand, given the state of confusion in France and the fact that Thorez himself was in Moscow, it was not clear that the communist hierarchy was in a position to control communist *maquisards*, many of whom undoubtedly did have revolutionary aspirations. All things considered, de Gaulle was probably not as certain of communist intentions as he suggested in his memoirs, and it was probably the very uncertainty that worried him.

In any case, he was relieved to learn, on 22 August, that Eisenhower had given orders for the French 2nd Armoured Division, commanded by General Leclerc, to head for Paris. On the morning of 25 August Leclerc entered Paris. De Gaulle himself arrived a few hours later. His arrival on that day and the events of the day after – in particular, the triumphant procession down the Champs Elysées – were the culmination of his rise to national leadership. The metaphor that French historians often use is that of a popular consecration, the public legitimization of a king who had claimed his throne *in absentia*.

. . .

In the context of de Gaulle's subsequent career, it would be difficult to exaggerate the significance of the war years. Those years had established – or perhaps one should say clarified – his entire political agenda. He may not have returned to Paris in 1944 with all his answers to France's problems fully formed, but he had at least decided what the problems were. There were essentially two. First of all, there was the problem that had been at the root of France's defeat in 1940 – the decay of the republican state, which had been so powerfully symbolized by the Third Republic's abdication to Pétain in July 1940. The primary task that de Gaulle set for himself in 1944 and to which he devoted the rest of his political life was the reconstitution of the French state into a state that could unite the nation, mobilize its energies, provide vigorous leadership, and stabilize France's erratic course through the twentieth century.

The ultimate responsibility of the state, in de Gaulle's view, was to protect and improve the position of France in the world. De Gaulle returned to Paris firmly convinced that the defeat of Germany would end one threat to

French prestige and power, but leave other, equally serious threats to be met. His difficult relations with Roosevelt only confirmed his realist's intuition that, beneath its idealistic rhetoric, the United States planned to establish its domination throughout the non-communist world. His observation of the way in which after 1942 Churchill took on the role of Roosevelt's faithful second left him with long-lasting suspicions of Britain's priorities. The Gaullist characterizations of the US as covert imperialist and Great Britain as apologetic accomplice had their roots in the war.

In addition, the war years had turned de Gaulle himself into a national leader and given him a unique symbolic identity, and yet had left him an inexperienced politician without an organized or cohesive following. In June 1940 he had risen to a position of leadership as a result of extraordinary circumstances, to a degree by default (because better-known people had either rallied to Pétain or done nothing), and certainly without having served a normal political apprenticeship. He had been compelled to step outside all hierarchy, political or military, and improvise an alternative state, whose legitimacy was indissociable from his own legitimacy.

Thereafter, he gradually redefined his mission from that of a soldier refusing to accept capitulation to that of a symbol not merely of continuing military resistance to Germany but of political resistance to Vichyism and Nazism. However, he did so without conceding a share in his legitimacy to the Resistance inside France and without confining himself to the role of the Resistance's leader. There were some Gaullists, like Brossolette, who hoped, in the light of the apparent ideological convergence between the General and the Resistance in 1942–43, that Gaullism might evolve into a permanent political movement, a broad progressive 'rally' ('rassemblement') to replace the discredited political parties of the Third Republic. De Gaulle refused this role for himself and effectively thwarted the chances of a Gaullist party by introducing the old political parties into the CNR in mid-1943. At the time there were compelling strategic reasons for making this decision, but its long-term effect – as we shall see, a rather momentous one – was to leave de Gaulle a symbolic leader rather than the head of a partisan movement.

The final year of the Occupation did not fundamentally alter this status. His Algerian initiation into the trials and tribulations of democratic politics was deceptive, because the circumstances in 1943–44 were so artificial: mainland France was still occupied; disagreements and divergences were temporarily effaced by the common goal of liberation; the CFLN was unconstrained by any constitutional procedures except those which it itself acknowledged. De Gaulle was able to be flexible in meeting the demands for democratic participation because he could feel that he was making concessions on his own terms. He worked with the CNR, the Provisional Consultative Assembly, the political parties, and the resistance movements, but he continued to insist that he was accountable only to the French people, who would make their will known after liberation.

In short, the war had schooled de Gaulle in certain kinds of politics – in the power politics of international relations and in the image-building and propagandizing of plebiscitary politics. But it had not really exposed him to the form of politics that he was about to encounter again in France – parliamentary politics. The transition from symbol to politician was to be far more protracted and painful than the transition from soldier to symbol had been in 1940.

. . .

NOTES AND REFERENCES

1. LNC vol. 3 pp. 65–7.
2. Lacouture J 1984 *De Gaulle* (3 vols). Le Seuil, Paris, vol. 1 pp. 428–31.
3. LNC vol. 3 p. 128.
4. Kersaudy F 1982 *Churchill and de Gaulle*. Collins and Atheneum, New York, pp. 136–44.
5. Kersaudy F 1982 pp. 161–7, 179–82.
6. De Gaulle C 1954 *Mémoires de guerre* (3 vols). Plon, Paris, vol. 1 p. 209.
7. LNC vol. 4 pp. 270–1.
8. Duroselle J-B 1982 *L'Abîme 1939–1945*. Imprimerie Nationale, Paris, pp. 401–2.
9. Kersaudy F 1982 pp. 233–4.
10. Letter of 23/1/43, LNC vol. 4 pp. 505–7.
11. Kaspi A 1971 *La Mission de Jean Monnet à Alger, mars-octobre 1943*. Editions Richelieu, Paris.

12. De Gaulle raconté par Maurice Schumann, *En ce temps-là de Gaulle* 54: 27.
13. 1979 *'L'Entourage' et de Gaulle*. Plon/Institut Charles de Gaulle, Paris, pp. 41–57.
14. Guichard J-P 1985 *De Gaulle et les mass media*. France-Empire, Paris, pp. 31–5.
15. Telegram of 8/7/41, LNC vol. 3 pp. 384–5.
16. De Gaulle C 1954 vol. 1 p. 214.
17. Guichard J-P 1985 p. 72.
18. Pineau C 1960 *La Simple Vérité, 1940–1945*. Julliard, Paris, pp. 152 ff.
19. Telegram of 9/6/43, LNC vol. 5 p. 24.
20. Shennan A 1989 *Rethinking France: Plans for Renewal, 1940–1946*. Oxford, pp. 53–68.
21. Telegrams of 6/6/44 and 10/6/44, LNC vol. 5 pp. 232–4, 240–1.
22. LNC vol. 5 p. 275.
23. Duroselle J-B 1982 p. 521.

Chapter 3

1944–46: LIBERATOR

1814 . . . When the Marquis of Maisonfort came to give his master the news of the events in Paris, he cried out joyously: 'Sire! You are king of France!' Louis XVIII replied coldly: 'Have I ever ceased to be?'[1]
1944 . . . As I was preparing to leave, Georges Bidault cried out: 'General! Here, around you, are the National Council of the Resistance and the Parisian Liberation Committee. We ask you solemnly to proclaim the Republic before the people gathered here.' I replied: 'The Republic has never ceased to exist . . . Why should I proclaim it?'[2]

. . .

In the early evening of 25 August 1944, a few hours after he had arrived in liberated Paris, de Gaulle stood at a window of the Hôtel de Ville and acknowledged the cheers of thousands of Parisians gathered down below. As he well knew, the people were cheering the symbol rather than the man. They scarcely knew the man – and, no doubt, curiosity was one of the things which brought them out into the streets to see him. The role of symbol had been a necessary and successful one for de Gaulle up to this point, but it would quickly become problematic. Under normal conditions of peacetime democracy, when there was no longer any pressing national crisis, the General could not remain a composite of values, images, and emotions. Sooner or later, he would have to flesh out his identity and define himself to the French people, by stating his views on difficult and often divisive issues. If he did not define himself, other politicians – naturally hostile ones – would do it for him. But could he define himself without demystifying himself, breaking the magical spell that united de Gaulle and France?

During the Occupation he had manipulated his symbolic stature, but in the aftermath of liberation there was a danger of becoming its prisoner. By taking on the role of representing France, he also took on the nation's internal contradictions and unresolved tensions. In the period after liberation the nation had highly confused and contradictory aspirations. On the one hand, it sought the national renewal that the Resistance and de Gaulle himself had talked about – a more egalitarian, modern, and productive society and a new republic. On the other hand, people naturally expected a return to prewar 'normality' – prewar living standards, the old way of life, and elements, at least, of the old political system. De Gaulle was perceived and perceived himself as the incarnation of both revolution and restoration. As the man who had emerged to lead France out of the abyss of June 1940, he could hardly countenance a return to the errors that had brought about the débâcle. But he was too familiar with – and, in truth, too sympathetic to – the enduring traits and traditions of the French past to believe in the revolutionary Utopia glimpsed by some resisters. As he put it to a prominent resister shortly after the liberation, France was not a country just beginning, but a country continuing.[3]

The most striking fact about de Gaulle's actions in the six months after the liberation of Paris was how little his priorities shifted, in contrast to those of the political class as a whole. While the war continued, and until early 1945 continued on French soil, the General's main concerns remained to secure the authority of his state, to maximize the French military contribution in the war against Germany, and to ensure as large a role as possible for France in the formulation of the peace settlement. In pursuing these aims, de Gaulle continued to find himself at odds with the British and Americans.

There were basically two sources of conflict. The first was diplomatic. De Gaulle's diplomatic objective was to restore France to the circle of great powers to which she had historically belonged. Though the three major Allies – the

United States, the Soviet Union, and Great Britain – were willing to concede this parity on occasion, the very act of *conceding* it demonstrated that it did not in reality exist. In fact, the Big Three continued to exclude de Gaulle from the most important inter-Allied conferences (at Dumbarton Oaks in the autumn of 1944 and at Yalta in February 1945). Exclusion from these conferences, and from various bilateral meetings among the leaders of the Big Three, was a source of considerable irritation to him. This irritation manifested itself most publicly in February 1945, when he refused an invitation to meet Roosevelt in Algiers immediately after Yalta, much to the annoyance of the Americans and the embarrassment of many at home. Apart from this kind of gesture, however, there was little that de Gaulle could do to get his way diplomatically.

He had a little more scope in the military arena, which was a second area of conflict with the Allies. Though the French army was utterly dependent on American supplies and was integrated into the inter-Allied command structure, de Gaulle was determined, whenever necessary, to protect French national interests. This attitude led to a number of clashes with Eisenhower. The first one occurred during the German counter-offensive in the Ardennes at the end of 1944, when Eisenhower ordered preparations for the evacuation of Strasbourg, which had only just been liberated by Leclerc's Armoured Division. De Gaulle took the view that the potential damage to morale caused by evacuating Strasbourg outweighed any military advantage, and so he countermanded Eisenhower's orders. A few months later, a similar but still more serious disagreement occurred, when de Gaulle again overrode American commanders and ordered General de Lattre to cross the Rhine (as the British and American armies were doing) and take Stuttgart. This led to a military standoff between French and American troops and a bitter rebuke from President Truman. Such conflicts spilled over into the immediate postwar phase. In May and June 1945 de Gaulle clashed with the Americans over the presence of French troops in Alpine regions that had belonged to Italy before the war. He also became embroiled in another conflict with Britain over Syria and Lebanon.

On the domestic front, de Gaulle's major priority in the

months after liberation was to secure his government's authority inside France, as against elements within the Resistance (communist or otherwise) who wanted to combine liberation with social revolution. The seriousness of this revolutionary threat has been the subject of intense debate, and historians have gradually moved to the view that it was not a likely outcome in the circumstances. But de Gaulle himself certainly took the danger seriously. To combat it, he made a series of important trips to the provinces in the autumn of 1944. These direct contacts with the people and with the maquis were intended to replicate the effect of his arrival in the capital, to demonstrate by his presence that the state had been restored. Back in Paris, he expanded his government into a government of national unanimity, including representatives of all the major parties and Georges Bidault, the head of the CNR. He swiftly integrated the 300,000 or so men of the Resistance army (the FFI) into the ranks of the regular army and disbanded a Resistance-run paramilitary force known as the *milices patriotiques*. With the assistance of his regional *Commissaires de la République*, he gradually contained undesirable local initiatives (such as the lynching of notorious collaborators and the illegal requisitioning of goods and *matériel*). By the end of November the Resistance had been domesticated, the leadership of the Communist Party (PCF) had fallen into line behind the government, and de Gaulle was in uncontested control of liberated territory. From that position of strength, he supervised the return of representative institutions. In early November, the Provisional Consultative Assembly was installed in its new surroundings in the Luxembourg Palace. Shortly afterwards the government announced the holding of the first post-liberation elections – municipal elections to take place in April and May of the following year.

During this first transitional phase, de Gaulle's preoccupations were mostly short-term. The only significant structural reform that he countenanced before the end of the war was the creation of consultative *comités d'entreprises* to provide for worker participation in factory management. This caution about tackling long-term problems, though very unpopular with the politicians and an impatient press, was obviously justifiable on practical grounds, so long as the war went on. De Gaulle could also justify it on grounds of principle. During the Occupation he had repeatedly declared that he would not anticipate the will of the French people. He could reasonably argue that only the nation could choose a permanent system of government and sanction fundamental structural changes in its society and economy.

With the municipal elections of April–May 1945 and the final surrender of the Germans on 8 May 1945, however, de Gaulle's government entered a new phase. The political life of the nation finally came out of its suspended animation. De Gaulle now had to deal with political parties reinvigorated by the return of elections and normal democratic processes. The short-term problems had by no means disappeared, but suddenly, with the end of the war, the mental horizons lifted, and politicians began to think with more urgency about the postwar future.

For de Gaulle, the future meant first and foremost the international settlement, particularly the all-important German settlement. De Gaulle had not waited for the end of the war to formulate his proposal for the new German settlement. In July 1944 he had told the American government and in December 1944 the Soviet government that the left bank of the Rhine ought to be detached from the rest of Germany and placed under French authority, while the Ruhr's industrial resources should be controlled by an international authority. Throughout his period in office, de Gaulle stuck to this line (and to the principle of a decentralized Germany), although he tried to make it more palatable by recasting it in terms of Germany's integration within a larger West European bloc.[4] This policy did not meet with success. When the leaders of the Big Three met at Potsdam in July 1945 (after again refusing to invite de Gaulle), they blocked de Gaulle's plans for the Ruhr and Rhineland. Worse still, from a Gaullist perspective, the Potsdam Conference moved in the direction of a centralized administration for Germany.

Undoubtedly this struggle to define the postwar settlement and preserve France's international position was uppermost in de Gaulle's thoughts in the summer and autumn of 1945. However, he also recognized that the domestic settlement could not be deferred much longer.

Mid-1945 was an important period of transition for him. He still refused to share his legitimacy with the parties, as he had refused to share it with the CNR. He still insisted that he alone was responsible to the French people for the actions of his government and would remain so until general elections could be held. But the challenges to his monopoly of legitimacy were becoming harder to dismiss. As the municipal elections had shown, the political parties (especially the parties of the left) enjoyed the confidence and support of a large section of the population, something which had not been the case with Giraud in 1943.

In the summer of 1945 he began to make more use of the enormous scope that the interim regime gave him to shape the future of the country. Rather than talking in general terms about the desirability of renewal, he began to talk in concrete terms of a timetable. In a radio address on 24 May, for example, he announced three major categories of reform, which he expected to see accomplished before the end of the year: reform of the civil service; nationalization of the coal, electricity, and banking industries; and a plan to boost France's birthrate. Around the same time, he acted to set the procedure of constitutional reform in motion. On 2 June, he was asked about this subject at a press conference. In the memoirs he recollected his response as follows:

> Three solutions are conceivable. Return to the bad old ways, elect separately a Chamber and a Senate, then bring them together at Versailles in a National Assembly which would or would not modify the Constitution of 1875. Or take the view that this constitution is dead and proceed to elections for a Constituent Assembly which would do whatever it saw fit. Or, finally, consult the country on the terms which would serve as a basis for determining its wishes and to which its representatives would have to conform.[5]

Characteristically, de Gaulle sharpened the contrasts in retrospect: the actual text of his comments made his own preference (for the third option) much less transparent.[6] But it was indeed his preference. In early July he formally announced his decision. General elections were to be held in October and were to be accompanied by a two-part referendum. The first part would ask voters whether they wanted a new republic or a return to the Third Republic. The second question – relevant only if a majority preferred a new constitution – asked voters to approve certain ground rules for the Constituent Assembly: a limited term, the obligation to submit its draft to another referendum, a clear separation of powers between the assembly and the provisional government whose president it would select. De Gaulle's plan touched off the first major political storm of the postwar era, which rumbled on throughout the rest of the summer. The parties accused de Gaulle of preparing a plebiscite; the General accused them of coveting an irresponsible, omnipotent assembly. The mounting criticism of the parties did not deter de Gaulle, however, and on 21 October 1945 the election-referendum went ahead as planned.

This election inaugurated the final phase of de Gaulle's period in office. On the surface, it was a propitious inauguration. De Gaulle had publicly expressed his preference for a 'yes-yes' vote (i.e. 'yes' to a new constitution and 'yes' to limitations on the prerogatives of the Constituent Assembly). Ninety-six per cent of the voters followed his lead on the first question and two-thirds on the second. When the Constituent Assembly elected him President of the Provisional Government, eighty per cent of the public approved (according to an opinion poll).[7] The results were widely interpreted at the time as a personal vindication for the General.

In fact, however, de Gaulle's position was less secure than it appeared. First of all, in the elections to the assembly, the people had given a resounding vote of confidence to three parties, all of which were opposed to de Gaulle's constitutional principles. With 160 seats, the Communist Party became the largest single party in the new assembly. Together with the Socialist Party (142 seats) and a new Christian Democratic party called the Mouvement Républicain Populaire (152 seats), the PCF formed a bloc which effectively ruled out the possibility of any constitution that de Gaulle could approve. More fundamentally still, the elections ended de Gaulle's monopoly of legitimacy. The sovereign people had given de Gaulle a vote of confidence, but they had also given a mandate to parties which opposed him. From that moment on, a split between de Gaulle and the parties was probably inevitable. The only way in which it could have been avoided was for de Gaulle to change his style of leadership. Until now he had never had to court the approval of the political elite, because his monopoly of legitimacy had made him irreplaceable. As soon as he became President of the Provisional Government by the vote of an assembly, he became eminently replaceable.

The final two months (November 1945–January 1946) were a miserable coda to de Gaulle's first period in office, as he confronted his new vulnerability. The task of constitution-making immediately passed beyond his control into the hands of the Constituent Assembly. The snubs and indignities that he received from that quarter have passed into Gaullist lore: when he so much as enquired about the progress of the assembly's constitutional commission, one of his own former ministers told him it was none of his business.[8] Emboldened by their mandate from the voters, the parties challenged de Gaulle at every turn. In November the communists objected to his practice of reserving the right to nominate particular people for particular ministries. In December the socialists challenged the executive's control over the budgetary process. He was able to overcome these and other challenges, but only by turning each issue into a question of confidence. Resignation threats had long been a weapon in de Gaulle's armoury, but in the past he had used them from a position of strength. Now he was appealing for the confidence of politicians, not for the confidence of the people. The politicians had trapped him into a game played by their rules. The realization of this fact quickly persuaded him to get out of the game before he lost whatever remained of his symbolic stature. On 20 January 1946, he resigned.

. . .

The record of de Gaulle's provisional government was a mixed one, in a sense both more creditable and less creditable than he himself suggested. His resignation letter focussed on his most basic achievements since liberation: the restoration of democracy and public order; the starting-up of the economy; the reconstitution of France's national territory and possessions.[9] At the time, his letter was criticized for what one Gaullist called its 'artificial optimism'.[10] In January 1946 bread rationing had recently been re-introduced, the franc had just been devalued, inflation was galloping, and Indochina was in crisis. It did not seem to people that, to use de Gaulle's expression, 'the train was back on the tracks'.[11] But for all its forced and rather infuriating serenity, the letter's tone was partially warranted, if one thinks of all that France and de Gaulle had been through since June 1940. He had indeed returned the nation to a semblance of domestic normality and international standing. There had been no civil war, no revolution, no dismemberment of French territories. In essence, he had accomplished his original mission.

Missing from the letter, however, was any mention of the reform efforts of the previous eighteen months – a record which one recent historian has fairly characterized as 'a more significant advance on the past than Labour's creditable six-year record in post-war Britain'.[12] De Gaulle's provisional government had renovated and extended the French welfare state. It had approved Jean Monnet's proposal for a Commissariat Général au Plan, the institution whose economic plans were to play an important role in France's postwar modernization. It had nationalized the coalfields of the Nord and Pas-de-Calais, the Bank of France, the four largest clearing banks, and the Renault and Gnome-et-Rhône companies. It had established the Ecole Nationale d'Administration for the training of elite civil servants, and had instituted worker participation schemes in the comités d'entreprises. Even though most of these reforms benefited from widespread political and public support, de Gaulle had played a critical role in bringing them to fruition.

On the other side of the ledger, de Gaulle also ignored some substantial failures and disappointments, above all in economic and foreign policy. In economic affairs, his most serious failure had been his reluctance to back Pierre Mendès-France in a vital policy debate inside the government in late 1944 and early 1945. Mendès-France, the Minister of National Economy, had proposed to head off impending inflation by cutting the money supply. His rigorous policy, which would have blocked bank accounts and exchanged old bank notes for new ones at something less than one-to-one, was resisted by a group of ministers led by the Minister of Finance, René Pleven. Pleven advocated a more liberal route (essentially an appeal to business and consumer confidence) without any forced reduction in the money supply. De Gaulle opted for Pleven's solution, on the grounds that the medicine that Mendès-France prescribed was too strong for a nation that was still recovering from its wounds.[13] Undoubtedly, part of the reason that this decision has attracted so much comment is that it was a rather 'un-Gaullist' one: for once, the General took the route of *facilité* rather than that of *inflexibilité*.[14] In terms of economic rationality, most experts now agree that Mendès-France was right and that the inflation which plagued France for years after 1945 might have been limited, if not avoided, by timely action by de Gaulle. De Gaulle's argument against Mendès-France was essentially the same that he had used against Eisenhower in Strasbourg a few months earlier: circumstances matter.

The other area where his record was vulnerable to criticism was that of foreign policy. In his memoirs he was, as ever, unapologetic about his policy of *grandeur* (greatness). On its own terms, his argument is virtually irrefutable: since *grandeur* was not a definable objective so much as a means of keeping the flame of national ambition alight, it could never really fail. From a non-Gaullist perspective, however, de Gaulle's policy clearly failed. Its only significant achievements came at the outset, when the Great Powers recognized the legitimacy of de Gaulle's government and invited France to become a permanent member of the United Nations Security Council – a status which would almost certainly not have been offered, had there been no de Gaulle and no Free France.[15] Beyond that, de Gaulle's policy failed both in a narrow and a broad sense. In the narrow sense, it failed to achieve its specific aims. For example, de Gaulle's December 1944 meeting with Stalin, which led to the signing of a Franco-Soviet pact, did not bring any substantial diplomatic advantage to France (although it did have favourable domestic repercussions). Stalin's attitude towards France remained as contemptuous after he had signed the pact as it had been before. It was he more than Roosevelt who barred de Gaulle from the

Yalta Conference. Equally abortive was de Gaulle's German policy. The General had no success in winning over the Big Three to his concept of a decentralized Germany, and he was excluded from the critical summits where Germany's future was discussed.

In a broader sense, de Gaulle's attitudes towards Germany and towards the empire (which he wanted to see reconstituted in a reformed imperial federation) were fundamentally at odds with the dynamics of the postwar world. In retrospect, we can see that de Gaulle was leading France into a cul-de-sac in 1946. One might argue, indeed, that his departure from power was a blessing in disguise for him, because it left others with the disagreeable but unavoidable job of extricating France from this cul-de-sac, by recognizing a powerful West German state and ultimately accepting German rearmament, by fighting and then retreating from a bloody colonial conflict in Indochina.[16] Perhaps de Gaulle was enough of a pragmatist to have made those adjustments himself, had he remained in power. But it is also possible that (as he once hinted in a press conference) he might have refused Marshall Aid rather than cave in to Anglo-American pressure on the German issue.[17] In that case the cost to France's economic reconstruction would have been immense.

There were fatal incongruities about *grandeur* in the circumstances of 1944–46. One was the incongruity between de Gaulle's ambitions and the needs of a nation on the breadline. Although the French public was susceptible to patriotic rhetoric and to comforting illusions about France's place in the world,[18] it did not share de Gaulle's sense of priorities. The issues that preoccupied most French citizens were domestic, not foreign: the punishment of collaborators, the food supply, the reconversion of the economy, prices and wages.

Another incongruity was that between de Gaulle's ambition and the resources at his disposal. *Grandeur* required military force, and force was expensive. A country desperately short of dollars and in need of total reconstruction could scarcely afford large military expenditures. De Gaulle had to recognize that himself: three times in 1945 he approved reductions in the military budget.[19] But when the socialists proposed a further cut at the end of 1945, he baulked. The budget debate that took place in the Constituent Assembly on New Year's Eve and New Year's Day is famous primarily for de Gaulle's veiled resignation announcement.[20] The issue at stake – as he phrased it – was institutional: who governs, the government or the assembly? But, as Robert Frank has convincingly argued, there was also a substantive issue.[21] The socialists maintained, with some justification, that the only way in which real *grandeur* could be achieved was through long-term economic modernization. For de Gaulle, however sympathetic to modernization in the abstract, there was a point beyond which resources could not be diverted from the immediate needs of his foreign policy in areas such as Germany and Indochina. That point had been reached. Again, one may be forced to the conclusion that his departure was a blessing in disguise for him. Even if he had got the kind of constitution that he wanted, could he have stomached the long period of economic rebuilding – with all its attendant constraints – that lay ahead of France in 1946? The burdens of reconstruction made the late 1940s and 1950s particularly inappropriate for a policy of *grandeur*, whereas by 1958, when de Gaulle returned to power, France was in a much better position to afford Gaullist ambition.

. . .

If the governmental record of the liberation era had been decidedly mixed, in personal political terms this period seemed an almost unmitigated disaster for de Gaulle. From the heady acclaim of August 1944, his popularity descended so far that his resignation provoked surprise but no emotion – a mere twenty-seven per cent of the French people said they wanted him back.[22]

An argument can certainly be made that de Gaulle had been the victim of circumstance. However often he and his ministers warned the population not to expect an overnight return to prewar prosperity, the head of the government was naturally held accountable for the persistence of food and fuel shortages, black marketeering, and bread rationing. Similarly, the settling of accounts with those who had collaborated (the *épuration*) was bound to be a messy and divisive process, whose excesses of lenience or harshness were inevitably blamed on de Gaulle. In general, it might be argued that the euphoric expectations of the liberation rebounded against him. As the euphoria had gone along with an irrational faith in the Gaullist saviour, so the deepening disillusionment of 1945, essentially an adjustment to reality, was reflected in a desanctification of the saviour figure.

On the other hand, there were steps which de Gaulle might have taken in 1944–46 – steps which might have produced a better outcome on the (to him) all-important issue of the constitution and might also have bolstered his popularity. In retrospect, for example, many Gaullists concluded that he should have formed a Gaullist movement of the kind that he formed, too late, in 1947 – a movement that could have channelled popular adulation into usable political support.[23] The idea of a Gaullist party had certainly been raised in the aftermath of the liberation – mostly by ex-resisters without a party affiliation[24] – but there is no evidence that de Gaulle gave it any more serious consideration than he had done in 1943. He was still too attached to his national status to risk it by appearing partisan. As he put it to one of his regional officials: 'If Joan of Arc had married and had children, she would not have been Joan of Arc any more.'[25]

The other path that he might have followed would have involved a direct appeal to the French people to support his constitutional views. One of the mysteries of this period is why he waited until five months *after* he had left office to describe his vision of a new republic to the voters. If he had given the speech that he gave at Bayeux in June 1946 a year earlier, he could have turned the October 1945 referendum and elections into a referendum on his own views. Or – as Michel Debré and others recommended – he could have presented a draft constitution to the people for approval, as he later did in 1958.

There are various explanations for his reluctance to do so. Perhaps he was still groping towards a fully-formed constitutional blueprint. Perhaps he was concerned about appearing to duplicate Pétain's unilateral constitutional revolution of 1940. Perhaps he was distracted by the war and by the pressing international issues. But probably his overriding motive was the concern to preserve a symbolic integrity by scrupulously honouring the pledge that he had often made during the war to allow the French people to choose their own institutions.

The concern with his symbolic, national status was the connecting thread of all de Gaulle's actions during the liberation period. His main aim in these months was to reconcile and renew the nation: hence no revolution, but most of the reforms that the CNR had wanted; hence a purge, but not the wholesale purge of all who had had dealings with the Germans or with Vichy; hence a referendum and free elections, but no plebiscite (whatever his opponents alleged, the referendum of October 1945 was not a true plebiscite); hence the presidency but no Gaullist party. Ultimately, de Gaulle's attempt to hold on to the symbolic status bestowed by 18 June and the war proved his undoing. In attempting to reconcile all segments of French society, he satisfied none. The resisters were more offended by de Gaulle's attack on their autonomy and by his restoration of the state apparatus than they were mollified by his reforms. Business and the bourgeoisie soon overcame their initial gratitude at being spared revolution and began to grumble about the 'collectivism' of de Gaulle's economic policies, not to mention the inclusion of communists in his government. The politicians were less impressed by the restoration of free elections than irritated by de Gaulle's determination to place constraints on the assembly's freedom of action.

In 1944–46 de Gaulle confronted the hard reality that a man of character could lead the nation singlehandedly in a moment of supreme crisis but not in normal times. He failed to make the necessary adjustments to his style of leadership – most obviously, to create some kind of transmission belt between himself and the nation. This failure could be explained as the product of political inexperience. It could also be explained as the product of pride – a disdain for integrating himself into any kind of partisan organization. If so, this was a species of pride which he subsequently overcame, no doubt partly as a consequence of his sobering experiences during this time. Or, finally, his failure to adapt himself in 1944–46 could be seen as the product of a genuine idealism. The mythic figure of the General – as portrayed in the *War Memoirs* – had known, from the moment he stood at the top of the Champs Elysées on

26 August 1944, that the new leaders whom the war had brought to power would betray the cause of national renewal. But it may well be that, to a degree that he would never have admitted, de Gaulle the politician had shared in the optimistic illusions of the liberation.

. . .

NOTES AND REFERENCES

1. Bertier de Sauvigny G de 1955 *La Restauration.* Flammarion, Paris, p. 55.
2. De Gaulle C 1956 *Mémoires de guerre* (3 vols). Plon, Paris, vol. 2 p. 308. The echoes of 1814 in 1944 are noted in Johnson D 1965 'The Political Principles of General de Gaulle'. *International Affairs,* **41** (4): 657.
3. Lacouture J 1985 *De Gaulle* (3 vols). Le Seuil, Paris, vol. 2 p. 32.
4. DePorte A 1968 *De Gaulle's Foreign Policy 1944–1946.* Harvard, Cambridge Mass., pp. 153–213, 251–76.
5. De Gaulle C 1959 *Mémoires de guerre* vol. 3 p. 256.
6. DM vol. 1 pp. 571–2.
7. Charlot J 1971 *Les Français et de Gaulle.* Plon, Paris, p. 31.
8. De Gaulle C 1959 p. 281.
9. De Gaulle C 1959 pp. 645–6.
10. Mauriac C 1978 *Le Temps immobile: aimer de Gaulle.* Grasset, Paris, p. 228.
11. Vendroux J 1974 *Cette chance que j'ai eue . . .* Plon, Paris, p. 161; DM vol. 2 p. 7.
12. Larkin M 1988 *France since the Popular Front.* Oxford, p. 128.
13. De Gaulle C 1959 p. 120.
14. De Gaulle C 1959 pp. 426–36.
15. DePorte A 1968 pp. 279–80.
16. Kolodziej E 1990 De Gaulle, Germany and the Superpowers: German Unification and the End of the Cold War. *French Politics and Society* **8** (4): 45.
17. Press conference of 17/11/48, DM vol. 2 p. 231.
18. Rioux J-P 1980 *La France de la Quatrième République* (2 vols). Le Seuil, Paris, vol. 1 p. 122.
19. Frank R 1983 Les Crédits militaires: contraintes budgétaires et choix politiques, in *De Gaulle et la nation face aux problèmes de défense (1945–1946).* Plon, Paris, p. 177.
20. Charlot J 1983 *Le Gaullisme d'opposition 1946–1958.* Fayard, Paris, pp. 38–9.
21. Frank R 1983 pp. 181–5.
22. Charlot J 1971 pp. 27, 199.

23. Astoux A 1974 *L'Oubli: de Gaulle 1946–1958*. J-C Lattès, Paris, pp. 72, 78.
24. Mauriac C 1978 pp. 41–2.
25. Bertaux P 1973 *Libération de Toulouse et sa région*. Hachette, Paris, p. 88.

Chapter 4

1946–58: THE POLITICS OF PROPHECY

It was during the course of his acrimonious exchanges with the Constituent Assembly on New Year's Day 1946 that de Gaulle evidently made up his mind to resign from the presidency. To avoid the impression that he was leaving in a fit of pique (and perhaps also to think through his decision more fully), he delayed the public announcement almost three weeks while he took a vacation in the South of France. This delay, combined with the lofty reassurances of his resignation statement, was apparently intended to project an impression of serenity. If so, it backfired disastrously. His opponents portrayed him as running away from the critical problems that the nation still confronted. For his supporters, the resignation was an embarrassing puzzle: why had he resigned so soon after accepting the presidency, as a result of a quarrel with a 'system' that he had largely created, over constitutional principles whose significance he had never bothered to explain to the French people?

The reasoning behind the unpopular and disastrous resignation immediately became the subject of intense speculation. Many suspected that it was a tactical manoeuvre. According to this view, de Gaulle was calculating that his resignation would produce a groundswell of popular annoyance with the parties or would give the politicians an opportunity to display their full incompetence – either of which outcomes would lead to de Gaulle's rapid reinstatement, this time with a popular mandate to create the kind of constitution that he favoured. On balance, the evidence does not support this tactical scenario, although it may well have occurred to de Gaulle. Most of those who saw the General in the weeks after his resignation did not come away with the impression that he was on the edge of his seat waiting to be asked back.[1] The consensus of Gaullist historians is that the resignation was meant seriously. By January 1946 de Gaulle had been brought face to face with the reality that a basic incompatibility of outlook and temperament existed between himself and the members of the assembly. As the walls of the political world closed in on him, the old imperative of *réserve* – his instinctive aversion for being hemmed in – reasserted itself. Undoubtedly, this claustrophobia was intensified by a growing sense that critical events were taking place elsewhere in the world, events which would shape France's future far more than would the decisions of the Constituent Assembly. De Gaulle was thinking in terms of a Third World War.[2] The threat of another war only made it more urgent for him to preserve his symbolic status, so that he could be the French people's supreme recourse should catastrophe strike once again.

Far from being the aberration that many Gaullists thought – and that, for years after, they were at a loss to explain – the departure of 1946 was utterly consistent with de Gaulle's conception of leadership. This, too, had been predicted in *The Edge of the Sword*:

> The price they [men of character] have to pay for leadership is unceasing self-discipline, the constant taking of risks, and a perpetual inner struggle. The degree of suffering involved varies according to the temperament of the individual; but it is bound to be no less tormenting than the hair shirt of the penitent. This helps to explain those cases of withdrawal which, otherwise, are so hard to understand. It constantly happens that men with an unbroken record of success and public applause suddenly lay the burden down.[3]

After five and a half years of intense activity the burdens of leading the French people had worn de Gaulle down. By the beginning of 1946 the national consensus that he had presided over at the liberation was visibly disintegrating. De Gaulle was losing control over the direction of political developments, and his prestige was draining away with every piece of bad economic news or foreign policy failure.

He was revolted by the paltry game that he was being forced to play in the assembly and increasingly sure that a greater game awaited him. As he put it to his son Philippe in February 1946: 'one cannot be both the man for great storms and the man for squalid deals.'[4]

De Gaulle followed his mysterious departure with a deafening silence. While the three major parties closed ranks to form a tripartite government and the assembly drafted a new constitution along the lines that de Gaulle had feared, he himself made no public appearances. In private it would seem that he was becoming increasingly fixated on the idea of a Third World War. His personal secretary, Claude Mauriac, recorded that the General was reverting, with some morose satisfaction, to the prophetic role of the 1930s and the early war years. In March he told Mauriac that there was bound to be a war between the Soviet Union and the 'Anglo-Saxons'. In April he told him that the next war had already started.[5] These premonitions increased in frequency as the summer wore on. In August, for example, de Gaulle predicted that the US would resort to force, once it became clear that Stalin was going to try to build atomic weapons.[6] The belief that sooner or later there would be another national emergency, which would force the nation to turn once again to him, was fundamental to de Gaulle's strategy throughout the long years of opposition between 1946 and 1958.

It was not, however, the sole dimension of his strategy. Just as the interwar prophet of Blitzkrieg had also been a lobbyist for the professional army, so, in the late 1940s and early 1950s, de Gaulle was not content simply to wait for disaster to strike. In June 1946, a month after a popular referendum had voted down the Constituent Assembly's proposed constitution and sent the parties back to the drawing board, de Gaulle re-entered the political fray. He did so in a speech in the Norman town of Bayeux – a symbolic location because this town had been one of those that he had visited in his first trip to liberated territory in June 1944. It is no exaggeration to say that the Bayeux speech established a new direction for postwar Gaullism. It indicated a willingness to descend to the political arena in circumstances other than those of national crisis. In so far as it explained his personal ideology to the French people, it may be regarded as the first speech of de Gaulle the politician, as opposed to de Gaulle the symbol. The message of de Gaulle the politician was that national renewal did not have to succeed national disaster; it could be achieved through a reform in the organization of the French state. He proposed a constitutional system in which the executive and legislative branches of government would be totally separate, in which the executive would be headed by a president above party politics and in a position to represent national unity and the long-term national interest, and in which the prime minister and ministers would be appointed by this president rather than by parliament. Here was a second dimension of Cold War Gaullism – a political, reformist dimension – to place alongside the prophetic, apocalyptic dimension.

The timing of the Bayeux speech – after the popular rejection of the first assembly's draft and before a second assembly got down to work – suggests strongly that de Gaulle made it with the aim of influencing the constitution-making process. Again, however, he was confronted by the problem which he had failed to overcome in 1945: how to translate popular support for his ideas into popular votes or votes in parliament? He may have hoped that the Christian democratic MRP would rally to a clearly articulated Gaullist constitution. After all, his links to Christian democracy went back a long way. The closest that the pre-war colonel had come to a political affiliation had been with progressive, Christian anti-fascists. On the eve of France's defeat, he had actually joined a group of this kind, the 'Amis de *Temps Présent*', some of whose members subsequently played a significant role in the Christian resistance and in the formation of the MRP.[7] For their part, the MRP leaders had presented their movement as the 'party of fidelity' (i.e. fidelity to de Gaulle) and had, in the end, opposed the first constitutional draft. If de Gaulle entertained hopes of an alliance, however, he was to be swiftly disappointed: the MRP did not endorse the Bayeux constitution and, instead, moved towards a compromise with the parties of the left.

Another option for the General was to sponsor an explicitly Gaullist movement. Such a movement had, in fact, been created in May 1946 by a left-wing Gaullist named

René Capitant. Capitant's Union Gaulliste apparently intrigued de Gaulle, but not enough for him to lend it active support or even sanction,[8] and de Gaulle's reluctance to throw his weight behind this initiative doomed it to failure. With the parties arrayed against him and no Gaullist movement to counter them, he was left with no means of influencing the constitutional debate in a positive direction. All that he could do was criticize the assembly's work from the outside. On four occasions (27 August, 19 September, 29 September, and 9 October) he publicly declared his opposition to the second assembly's draft, which he characterized as a barely modified version of the first. Although his opposition certainly influenced many voters, on 13 October 1946 the French people voted to approve the constitution of the Fourth Republic by a narrow majority, with thirty-two per cent of voters abstaining.

De Gaulle could legitimately claim that the result was the most lukewarm endorsement conceivable; this did not alter the fact that it marked a personal setback for him. Indeed, it was the culmination of a series of setbacks. He had waited too long to make his constitutional views known. Even after he had made them known, he had made it virtually impossible for voters to express their agreement with his views (by refusing to patronize the Union Gaulliste or some equivalent). He had failed to win back the support of the MRP. At the end of it all, France had precisely the kind of constitution that he had all along wanted to avoid. In December 1946 de Gaulle was further than ever from power, while the world was closer to war. It was one of the lowest points of his career – perhaps the lowest since Dakar in September 1940.

It was at this nadir that de Gaulle made the decision to create a new political movement, which he called the Rassemblement du Peuple Français (RPF – Rally of the French People). By any rational political calculation, the timing of this move could not have been worse. A Gaullist movement might have worked wonders in 1945 or 1946, but by 1947 de Gaulle's political opponents were firmly entrenched in power. It was difficult to see how the RPF would be able to advance the Bayeux agenda until the next legislative elections, which were scheduled for 1951. Furthermore, any movement basing itself on one man, with an ideology of systematic hostility to parliamentary politics and of vocal nationalism, was bound to be classified on the extreme right. The more de Gaulle insisted that his was not a party and that he was appealing to all patriotic men and women of every class, the more he was conforming to stereotypes of right-wing authoritarianism. There was a real danger that this adventure would reduce de Gaulle from the status of a truly national leader to the status of a right-wing ideologue.[9] Even by a Gaullist calculus, it appeared a very peculiar decision. Whatever de Gaulle said, any political organization which chose to operate within democratic constraints was likely to become a political party sooner or later. And what would this do to the myth of the great man in reserve? More than one Gaullist found himself in the difficult situation of having to give de Gaulle a lecture in Gaullism. Here, for example, was Claude Mauriac's advice: 'Time would be on de Gaulle's side, if only he consented to keep quiet. Sooner or later, events would see to his recall.'[10] Mauriac could only explain de Gaulle's decision as the product of impatience. If so, it was impatience of a singular kind – not just the feeling that he had something important to contribute, but the certainty that France (and the whole world) was on the verge of a colossal crisis and that he had to be ready. The timing of the RPF's creation was so unpropitious and the concept of a Gaullist 'party' so problematic even to de Gaulle that one must assume that he felt that he had no real choice. In his mind, France was in the phoney war all over again, and May 1940 was fast approaching. To Mauriac's lesson in Gaullist orthodoxy, de Gaulle replied: 'Politics have never been less inviting than at this moment. But I think I have no right not to try the impossible in order to save the country. I may not succeed, but I must try.'[11]

. . .

Though he devoted six years of his life to the RPF, de Gaulle virtually ignored it in his memoirs. Historians seem to have taken the lead from their subject: the RPF is still the least studied and least well-understood part of de Gaulle's career. Yet, in so far as it constituted his baptism as a politician, it is crucial to an understanding of his political career.

De Gaulle launched the Rassemblement in a speech at Strasbourg on 7 April 1947. Refusing to call the new creation a party, he defined it as a reincarnation of Free France – a non-partisan national reserve, open to all patriotic French men and women. It was necessary at this juncture because the parties controlling the new republic were inherently incapable of safeguarding French interests and sovereignty in the face of a looming world crisis. As an astute contemporary observed, 'the strange thing is that de Gaulle did not, at any time, suggest that he could save [the French people] from [war]; the suggestion was rather that if war was to come . . . it would be better for France if he were in charge'.[12]

From the outset, however, de Gaulle insisted on giving the Rassemblement a programme beyond 'de Gaulle au pouvoir'. The reformist dimension heralded at Bayeux immediately found a place in the RPF. The essence of this programme was constitutional reform, but, in addition, de Gaulle committed the Rassemblement to a theoretically radical scheme of profit-sharing and worker participation in management (which he termed 'association capital-travail') and to a vaguely-worded economic liberalism, whose aim was clearly to capitalize on popular frustration with the continuing economic hardships (1947 saw the bread ration reduced on two occasions). On all the imperial and foreign policy issues that arose over the succeeding years (the Cold War, Germany, the Atlantic Alliance, Indochina, Korea, the European Defence Community), he insisted on defining a 'party line'. This continual effort to expound a programme gave the Rassemblement somewhat greater legitimacy as a democratic movement, but it also made it seem very much a party like all the others.

So too did de Gaulle's early decision to take the Rassemblement into the electoral arena. In 1947 there was no likelihood of legislative elections in the near future, but various local elections lay ahead (with the first ones, municipal elections, scheduled for October 1947). Some of the RPF's leaders were uneasy about risking the new movement's reputation by contesting these elections, but de Gaulle, perhaps trying to make up for the lost opportunities of 1945 and 1946, was adamant that the Rassemblement should make an all-out effort to capture as much popular support as possible.[13] In the summer of 1947 de Gaulle manoeuvred to improve the RPF's electoral prospects. In particular, he modified the Rassemblement's message to reflect the onset of the Cold War, which had been marked inside France by the government's expulsion of its communist ministers in May 1947. In the wake of that event and of the international crisis associated with the announcement of the Truman doctrine and the Marshall Plan, de Gaulle added a pungent anti-communism to the original brew. At Rennes, on 27 July 1947, the *rassembleur* turned cold warrior: 'Soviet Russia is using coercion to organize around herself a formidable grouping of states . . . This bloc's frontier is separated from ours by no more than 500 kilometres, or just about two stages of the Tour de France!'[14] In sinister terms, de Gaulle now limited his appeal 'to all true Frenchmen', excluding the communist 'separatists' 'who do not play France's game'.

A frightened nation apparently found his message reassuring. In October forty per cent of voters supported the RPF, and more than half of France's largest cities (including Paris) elected a Gaullist mayor. On 27 October a triumphant de Gaulle claimed a popular mandate for the RPF and demanded that the National Assembly be dissolved. He was not interested in the compromise solution of becoming prime minister within the existing regime. That would have put him back in the situation of January 1946 – forced to swallow hard decisions in domestic and foreign policy without the long-term mandate to govern in the manner that he saw fit. For a moment, it appeared that his intransigence might pay off: many of his opponents in the MRP and Socialist Party were on the verge of losing their nerve and submitting to his ultimatum. In the end, however, the steadying influence of the President of the Republic, the socialist Vincent Auriol, helped the government ride out the storm. To cope with the Gaullist surge (and with the communist threat on their other flank), the centrist parties committed to the status quo made a virtue of necessity by banding together to form what they called the 'Third Force'.

Once the Fourth Republic had refused to imitate the Third Republic by committing suicide, de Gaulle had to face the problem of sustaining the Rassemblement's momentum. One option that he did not possess was the mass medium of radio which he had used so effectively during the war: in April 1947 the prime minister Paul Ramadier prohibited retransmission of de Gaulle's speeches. On only one occasion during the entire RPF period, shortly before the general elections of 1951, was de Gaulle given access to radio. To compensate for this handicap, which was compounded by the hostility of the mainstream press, de Gaulle and the RPF were compelled to make creative use of the assets that they did have. Their main asset was the General himself. Throughout the RPF years, he took his message to the French people in person. He visited every corner of the country. In one year alone (1950), he travelled to more than sixty *départements*. The highlight of these provincial tours was the set-piece political rally, for which the RPF became famous (or notorious). These rallies, which were not infrequently marked by violent clashes with communists, reminded many people of Hitler's Nuremberg rallies.[15] They were elaborately staged: flags and crosses of Lorraine decorated the podium; ex-resisters, locals dressed in traditional regional costume, and children carrying flowers were on hand to greet the General. Usually de Gaulle would be introduced by André Malraux, who would conclude with the phrase that had preceded de Gaulle's wartime broadcasts from London: 'Honneur et Patrie'. Then came the General's speech, which was the centrepiece of the rally. These RPF speeches had a repetitive but rousing formula: lyrical invocation of the heroism of Free France and the Resistance; violent denunciation of the Third Force, the malevolent PCF and the sinister and expansionist Soviet Union; and, finally, the Gaullist prescription for recovery. At the end de Gaulle would lead the assembled masses in a thunderous Marseillaise.

In addition to de Gaulle's trips and speeches, the RPF employed a variety of unconventional methods to publicize itself and keep its momentum. For example, in 1948 de Gaulle sponsored a so-called 'stamp campaign', in which citizens were invited to buy special 50-franc stamps and send them to the General's home in the village of Colombey-les-deux-Eglises. The aim of this campaign was twofold: both to raise money and, in the words of the RPF newspaper, 'to give once more a visible expression to the confidence that France has in [de Gaulle]'.[16] On both counts the campaign was successful. It produced 100 million francs and plenty of newsreel showing sacks of letters being unloaded in Colombey.

In spite of de Gaulle's efforts and the efforts of a growing organization (which, by 1948, had 400,000 members and almost two hundred affiliated parliamentarians),[17] the RPF's popularity gradually slipped from its 1947 levels. Contemporary opinion polls strongly suggest that the 1947 peak had been a product of Cold War hysteria, and that, as war fears eased in 1948 and 1949, some of the RPF's 'soft' support eroded. The decline was not drastic. After the outbreak of the Korean War in June 1950, the Rassemblement retained legitimate ambitions for victory in the legislative elections of June 1951. Despite moments of despondency, de Gaulle himself certainly did not give up hope. In February 1951, he wrote to his son: 'This year's elections will be good, I am sure of it.'[18] De Gaulle's opponents in the Third Force feared as much. To counter both the Gaullist and the communist threats, they passed a new electoral law, whose aim was to make it harder for the RPF or the PCF to win a majority. The new law retained proportional representation but gave considerable advantage to those parties which were willing to form pre-electoral coalitions (or *apparentements*) with other parties. It was a brilliant, if devious, strategem. The RPF was placed in an impossible dilemma. It could abandon its isolation and make deals with other parties – in which case it would contradict its own anti-party rhetoric and make itself indistinguishable from other parties. Or it could preserve its ideological purity and risk losing the elections. Some in the RPF leadership contemplated calling the Third Force's bluff and proposing *apparentements* with MRP candidates. But the General would have none of it: the last thing that he wanted was a tainted victory, with RPF delegates beholden to another party. For him, it was all or nothing.

The June 1951 elections did not mark the beginning of the end for the RPF. That had come in 1948, when the war scare had eased, the Third Force's resolve had stiffened, and American economic aid had begun to make itself felt. But the elections were a further, and fatal, blow. That may seem an unduly harsh judgement on a contest which, in some sense, the RPF 'won'. With 119 seats, the Rassemblement became the largest party in the new assembly. Without the system of *apparentements*, it would have won 143 seats.[19] But the reality was that the RPF had needed 200 or so seats to be in a position to force through constitutional reform and the return of de Gaulle. Without that leverage, the RPF could either take a vow of self-imposed isolation (in the hope that this would be rewarded by electoral victory in 1956) or risk its anti-system character by participating in parliamentary politics and even holding a share of power in coalition governments. The first option was politically impractical, as close advisers like Georges Pompidou realized.[20] The second option, which naturally held attractions for the RPF parliamentarians, was met with total scorn by de Gaulle. He insisted that if the RPF even took part in the charade of 'consultations' before the formation of a ministry, the public would cease to see any distinction between it and the rest.[21] He viewed all parliaments as swamps which suck down good and bad alike: 'nobody can achieve anything in parliament or through parliament.'[22]

That comment, made shortly after the 1951 elections, is sufficient to explain the split which gradually developed between the RPF parliamentarians and de Gaulle. This split first became public in early 1952, when a group of twenty-seven RPF parliamentarians broke ranks and gave a vote of confidence to the conservative prime minister Antoine Pinay. It culminated in May 1953 when the General severed links between the RPF and its deputies, and began to wind up the Rassemblement. In retrospect, this split was probably inevitable. What is surprising and interesting is not de Gaulle's disenchantment with the parliamentary game, which was hardly new, but the perseverance that he showed in sticking with the RPF. In 1951 and 1952 he continued to act as the Rassemblement's main spokesman, addressing rallies and holding press conferences. Even after the rebellion of the twenty-seven deputies, he intermittently held out some, albeit slim, hopes for the RPF. In May 1952, he told his brother-in-law Jacques Vendroux that he would keep the RPF alive at least until the middle of the legislature (1953 or 1954) so that he could gauge the prospects for the next elections.[23] The very fact that he held the parliamentarians partially responsible for the RPF's de-mise[24] suggests that he had not assumed in June 1951 that the Rassemblement was dead.

The diaries and memoirs of those who worked closely with de Gaulle in these years give the impression that his gradual disengagement from the RPF (which began in 1951 and was not complete until 1954) was not only more protracted but also more painful than his disengagement from the provisional government in January 1946. Louis Terrenoire, the RPF's general secretary in this era, saw de Gaulle as a tragic figure caught in an intolerable dilemma: 'should I remain the man of History . . . and withdraw? Or should I commit myself over and over again, and continue to be thought of as the leader of one political group among others?'[25] In the end there could only be one option for de Gaulle, but the time it took him to make the decision indicated how difficult it was. It was difficult to abandon the RPF precisely because de Gaulle had so compromised himself and his unique prestige by setting it up in the first place, by fighting elections, and by being a politician 'like the others'. Like a losing gambler, he found it difficult to walk away.

. . .

The RPF was indeed a gamble for de Gaulle. In retrospect it suggests, like many gambles, a kind of compulsive beha-viour. There was something compulsive about constantly superimposing the conditions of 1940 on 1947: a foreign menace (then Germany, now the USSR); an internal force playing the enemy's game (then Vichy, now the Commun-ist Party); a weak state blindly trusting all to its ally (then the Third Republic deferring to Great Britain, now the Fourth Republic deferring to the United States); a minority of clear-sighted patriots uniting to rescue the nation (then Free France, now the RPF). The RPF was a replica, or a parody, of Free France. On one occasion (24 April 1947) de Gaulle retrospectively renamed the wartime Resistance the rassemblement du Peuple Français, as though all he had done in 1947 was capitalize it. On another occasion (25 June 1950) he referred to the RPF as 'the second phase of our national task'. Before it became the populist anti-communist crusade of October 1947 or the parliamentary party of 1951, the RPF was a brotherhood of ex-resisters and Free Frenchmen bound to one another and to de Gaulle by nostalgia.

There was also something compulsive about the extremism of his rhetoric in the RPF era. His speeches conveyed an oppressively apocalyptic vision. The longer he was excluded from power, the darker became his premonitions. Here is a typical sentence from an RPF speech (18 June 1949): 'The new threat may not be far away; while the horizon darkens, we see those waves of baseness which often precede the hurricane . . .' Even when he was optimistic about the RPF's prospects, his vision and language were sombre, even somewhat threatening: the RPF was itself a wave, a huge cleansing wave coming from the depths of the national consciousness.

Similarly excessive were de Gaulle's vitriolic attacks on the politicians. It was almost as if he felt that they had made a fool of him in 1945–46 and was trying to atone for his naiveté. He exchanged the lofty ecumenism of the liberation for an extreme partisanship. One of the ironies of this was that he himself behaved more like a politician than at any other time in his career. How like a politician's were his constant attempts to justify his own record (for example, his decision to sign a pact with Stalin and to admit the 'separatists' into his governments in the mid-1940s) or to claim credit for 'successes' (such as the exclusion of the communist ministers in 1947) which belonged, in fact, to others. The grafting of anti-communism onto the RPF's ideology in the summer of 1947 was itself a highly political decision. That is not to say that it was pure opportunism. De Gaulle had long believed that the PCF's tendency to align itself with Moscow invalidated it in crucial respects, and in November 1945 he had refused to give the PCF one of the three ministries that he regarded as essential to national security. But the new emphasis on anti-communism in 1947 was tactically opportunistic in the sense that de Gaulle consciously manipulated the fear of communism to win votes. 'Only one thing could open the French people's eyes – fear,' he had told one of his former advisers shortly after resigning in 1946.[26] In 1947 he evidently realized that the best way of stimulating and tapping into popular fear was anti-communism.

Ultimately, de Gaulle's aim was not to destroy communism or to meet any other specific threat. It was to change the nature of France's regime, so that the nation would be better placed to meet any challenge or resolve any problem that it might have to face. Even if one accepted de Gaulle's implausible claim that the RPF had saved France from communism in 1947, it was clear by 1951 that the RPF had failed to achieve its essential aim, since the Fourth Republic had survived.

Was de Gaulle himself responsible for this failure? His leadership has been criticized in a number of particulars: the timing of the movement's creation (too early or too late); the adoption of anti-communism, which had short-term benefits but turned Gaullism into a right-wing preserve; the systematic hostility to parliament and refusal to negotiate with the parties; the tactical mistake of refusing *apparentements* in June 1951. There is some validity in most of these criticisms, but they should not obscure the fact that the fundamental problems with the RPF were conceptual rather than tactical or organizational. The Rassemblement had been premised on a total governmental collapse. This collapse did not materialize and, more to the point, by 1948 an increasing percentage of the French people no longer believed in the imminence of such a collapse. This left de Gaulle in the impossible situation of trying to keep up a wartime psychology, while the French people wanted to live a peacetime existence.[27]

He responded by falling back on a reformist, electoral strategy. At that point the contradictions between the two dimensions of Gaullism became apparent. How could a violently anti-system movement conceived for an extraordinary emergency akin to that of 1940 adapt to a gradualist parliamentary strategy? How could a man so constitutionally unsuited to parliamentary life lead his party to power through parliament? If either the elections or the crisis had come in 1947, then the contradiction probably would not have mattered. If de Gaulle had adopted an exclusively parliamentary approach, the RPF's victory in 1951 might have been enough to carry him back to power, but only on the system's terms. That was never a palatable option for the General. Nor was the other option of an exclusively extra-parliamentary mass movement. Some have seen the RPF as a twentieth-century expression of Bonapartism – the tradition of a providential leader appealing to men and women of all classes and ideologies to unite in the interests of an orderly state and national greatness.[28] Others view the RPF – with its anti-communism, nationalism, paternalistic anti-capitalism, and cult of the leader – in a more sinister light, as a quasi-fascist movement. The reality, however, was that, once the great crisis failed to appear, de Gaulle played out his hand in a conventional electoral fashion, because he saw no alternative to coming to power in that way. Though he sometimes raised the possibility of having to step outside normal channels if 'certain people were to stifle democracy',[29] this was just provocative rhetoric. His actions were not those of a revolutionary.

With the benefit of hindsight, historians have been able to find various silver linings for de Gaulle in the protracted failure of the RPF. They have noted that many of the men who built and ran the Fifth Republic cut their teeth in the RPF.[30] Members of this Gaullist elite also played an important role in engineering the General's return to power in 1958.[31] For de Gaulle himself, the experience taught valuable lessons, particularly about the dangers of being trapped in the role of party leader. When he finally returned to power, he was careful not to preside over the new Gaullist party, the UNR, in the same direct way that he had led the RPF.

It might also be argued that the RPF provided de Gaulle with a means of influencing popular and political opinion on critical issues, particularly those relating to foreign affairs. In the longer perspective, the RPF era was an important stage in the development of his international design. After a brief phase of unambiguous Atlanticism at the beginning of the Cold War, de Gaulle soon showed himself to be a cold warrior with one eye on the danger of 'le protectorat de Washington'. Many of the arguments that he was later to use in his campaign against integration of French forces in NATO were first rehearsed in speeches and press conferences between 1949 and 1954: for example, the unacceptability of a command structure that placed French troops and assets under non-French control; or the inherent unreliability of the American nuclear umbrella, once the USSR had acquired the bomb.

Similarly it was during the RPF years that the first significant evolution in de Gaulle's attitude towards Germany occurred. In 1947–48 he had continued to advocate a decentralized Germany, closer to the pre-1871 state than to the Weimar state of 1919. However, once West Germany had become a reality, he modified his position. While he continued to raise the spectre of a return to German hegemony, his new policy (voiced for the first time at Bordeaux in September 1949) revolved around a Franco-German entente, which he saw as the basis for a European confederation. This became the genesis of his German policy after 1958.

Finally, in criticizing the Fourth Republic's subservience not only in the Atlantic Alliance but also in the emerging institutions of European cooperation, de Gaulle defined more clearly (though far from unambiguously) his own vision of European unification. This vision had both a positive and a negative aspect. On the positive side, he advocated an economic, military, and cultural confederation of European nation-states, in which, by virtue of her large empire, France would play the leading role. On the negative side, he rejected absolutely any attempt to achieve European unity through supranational organizations such as the Coal and Steel Community or the European Defence Community. In his long and ultimately successful battle against the latter organization (a European army in which French, German, and other European units would have been integrated under American command) de Gaulle developed all his objections to supranationalism. Both the positive and the negative sides of Gaullist Europeanism were to re-emerge within the European Economic Community after 1958.

The end of the Rassemblement provoked bouts of disillusionment in de Gaulle, just as the resignation in 1946 had done. 'I have gone from failure to failure, with France, alas, the loser. Failure of the Armoured Corps . . . Failure at Dakar . . . Failure in 44 and 45 when I wanted to rally all Frenchmen together . . . Failure when I created the RPF.'[32] Yet, beneath this pessimism, de Gaulle retained faith in his historic destiny. If anything, his faith was strengthened in the mid-1950s, as he worked over the past to write his *War Memoirs*. He held his last press conference in 1955, but no more than in 1946 did he resign himself to a permanent retirement. To Louis Terrenoire, he cited the example of the nineteenth-century statesman Thiers, who had been Louis-Philippe's minister in 1840, and returned to power thirty-one years later.[33] To Jacques Vendroux, he confided:

> Our country will not tolerate much longer the weakness of those who are leading it . . . The tragedy in Algeria will doubtless produce an upsurge by the best Frenchmen. For more than thirty years I have been fighting for them. They know it. And even those who oppose me know it. It will not be long before they are obliged to come looking for me.[34]

The date was October 1957. Seven months later, his prediction came true.

. . . .

NOTES AND REFERENCES

1. Charlot J 1983 *Le Gaullisme d'opposition 1946–1958*. Fayard, Paris, pp. 40–1.
2. Letter of 7/11/45, LNC vol. 6 p. 111.
3. De Gaulle C 1960 *The Edge of the Sword* trans G Hopkins. Criterion Books, New York, pp. 65–6.
4. LNC vol. 6 p. 190.
5. Mauriac C 1978 *Le Temps immobile: aimer de Gaulle*. Grasset, Paris, pp. 264–5, 281–2.
6. Mauriac C 1978 p. 339.
7. Lacouture J 1984 *De Gaulle* (3 vols). Le Seuil, Paris, vol. 1 pp. 291–3.
8. Lacouture J 1985 *De Gaulle* (3 vols). Le Seuil, Paris, vol. 2 pp. 275–6.
9. Mauriac F 1964 *De Gaulle*. Grasset, Paris, p. 56.
10. Mauriac C 1978 p. 382.
11. Mauriac C 1978 p. 383.
12. Werth A 1956 *France 1940–1955*. Robert Hale, pp. 368–9.
13. Charlot J 1983 pp. 102–3.
14. DM vol. 2 p. 102.
15. Werth A 1956 p. 370.
16. Charlot J 1983 pp. 131-2.
17. Charlot J 1983 pp. 88, 163–4.
18. LNC vol. 6 p. 466.
19. Charlot J 1983 p. 238.

20. Pompidou G 1982 *Pour rétablir une vérité*. Flammarion, Paris, p. 133.
21. Terrenoire L 1981 *De Gaulle 1947–1954: pourquoi l'échec?*. Plon, Paris, p. 153.
22. Pompidou G 1982 p. 133.
23. Vendroux J 1974 *Cette chance que j'ai eue* . . . Plon, Paris, p. 330.
24. Vendroux J 1974 p. 346.
25. Terrenoire L 1981 p. 222.
26. Alphand H 1977 *L'Etonnement d'être*. Fayard, Paris, p. 194.
27. Touchard J 1978 *Le Gaullisme, 1940–1969*. Le Seuil, Paris, p. 107.
28. Guiol P 1985 *L'Impasse sociale du gaullisme: Le RPF et l'action ouvrière*. Presses de la FNSP, Paris, pp. 289–90.
29. Speech of 12/2/49, DM vol. 2 p. 259.
30. Charlot J 1983 p. 373.
31. Touchard J 1978 p. 133.
32. Michelet C 1981 *Mon père Edmond Michelet*. Robert Laffont, Paris, pp. 222–3.
33. Terrenoire L 1981 p. 297.
34. Vendroux J 1974 p. 433.

Chapter 5

1958: THE RETURN

De Gaulle's political career can be conceptualized in terms of two cycles, with the first stretching from 1940 to 1946, and the second from 1958 to 1969. (The anomalous episode of the RPF constitutes an abortive cycle in its own right.) In each cycle de Gaulle passed through three stages – the assumption of France, the period of recognition and power, and the final phase of withdrawal. By this logic, there was an essential parallel between his first assumption of France in 1940 and his second assumption in 1958. That was certainly how de Gaulle saw things:

> On 18 June 1940, answering the call of the eternal fatherland . . . de Gaulle, alone and almost unknown, had had to assume France. In the month of May 1958, on the eve of a disastrous tearing-apart of the nation and faced by the utter prostration of the system which was supposedly in charge, de Gaulle, now well-known but with no resource except his legitimacy, had to take destiny in his hands.[1]

De Gaulle had an obvious self-interest in pairing his controversial actions in May 1958 with the irreproachable initiative of June 1940. But despite a similar loss of faith in the republican regime and a similar loss of self-confidence within the regime, the two assumptions were, in crucial respects, far from identical.

To begin with, de Gaulle himself was a different person, not just eighteen years older, rounder in form and, by most accounts, mellower in temperament but also a man with a past – the symbol of 1940–44, the liberator of 1944–46, the politician of Bayeux, and the leader of the RPF. This history and experience shaped the way he was perceived by others. It also shaped his own priorities: in 1958, he returned not just with the aim of saving France's honour, but with a clear vision of a new regime that he intended to found as well as a hard-won wisdom about how best to realize his vision.

Secondly, the circumstances of his return were quite different from those of 1940. In 1958 the appeal to which de Gaulle responded came not from the 'eternal fatherland' submerged by foreign forces but from the European settlers and the French army in Algeria, elements of which were in open insurrection against the legal, democratic government. Under these circumstances, his intervention could not possibly be perceived as an unambiguously patriotic and non-partisan gesture.

Finally, the historical context was different. This time the crisis did not occur as part of a general European crisis threatening France's national survival. Nor did it follow a period of economic and demographic stagnation. On the contrary, it came in the course of a remarkable postwar recovery, which was transforming France into a modern, prosperous, and dynamic society. However serious the immediate crisis in 1958 might have been, it was not the same kind of international and societal breakdown that had taken place in 1940.

De Gaulle's letters in the months before his return stressed that he would take no further initiatives until the French people had demonstrated their disgust with the existing regime and their desire for a radical change. In the RPF years he had allowed himself to get ahead of events. In disengaging from that strategy and withdrawing to his study to memorialize the de Gaulle of history, the General reverted to his original concept of the leader-in-reserve – the solitary hero to whom the nation would inevitably turn in a moment of dire emergency.

The potential for a national emergency in the near future was unmistakeable. By 1957 almost half a million French troops, mostly young draftees or reservists but with a substantial leavening of Foreign Legionnaires and other regulars, were fighting a long and brutal war in Algeria against the forces of an independence movement known as the Front de Libération Nationale (FLN). France's stake in this conflict was enormous. Algeria occupied a unique place in the empire. It was the only colony under the direct jurisdiction of the Ministry of the Interior and, therefore, nominally at least, it was an integral part of France. It was home to a million or so settlers of European origin, the so-called *pieds noirs*. It was also France's largest colonial trading partner and possessed considerable oil and gas reserves.[2] The army that was fighting there, particularly its professional component, was still bruised by the defeat it had sustained in Indochina in the early 1950s and was determined not to repeat the experience. It saw the new enemy as a virtual replica of the old one, i.e. as a band of Marxist revolutionaries committed to the destruction of the Free World. As a result of this potent combination of sentiment and self-interest, the war had assumed the character of something more than a military operation: in the minds of the military and of many civilians, left and right, it had quickly become a decisive test of France's national will and international power.

In purely military terms, the army could feel that it was meeting the challenge in 1957 and early 1958. Using counter-insurgency techniques first learned in Indochina, it steadily reduced the level of FLN attacks. A fortified barrier constructed along the border between Algeria and Tunisia slowed the flow of troops and weapons to the enemy. In the city of Algiers the 10th Paratroop Division commanded by General Jacques Massu decimated the FLN organization, thanks, in part, to an extensive use of torture. However, the fact that the war could not be won outright was gradually sapping public confidence in the political objective of 'French Algeria'.[3] The war was also exerting severe strain on the metropolitan economy, damaging France's international reputation, and accentuating political divisions and governmental instability inside the regime. In short, the nation seemed to be heading inexorably towards an impasse. How to reconcile a Muslim majority sympathetic to nationalism with a settler minority convinced that Algeria was an integral part of France and morbidly afraid of being sold out by Paris? How to win a vicious guerrilla war without compromising the moral and political values that France claimed to represent? How to achieve a political settlement without antagonizing an army which had committed its honour to the goal of total, unconditional victory?

After 1956 – the year in which the government had tried and failed to cut off Arab support for the FLN in the ill-fated Anglo-French Suez expedition – there had been a growing perception, both in Paris and among the general public, that these dilemmas were not likely to be resolved by short-lived coalition governments of the kind that the Fourth Republic produced. As that fact sank in, more and more people thought of de Gaulle as a potential last resort. The Fourth Republic's president, René Coty, was among those who believed (as early as 1956) that de Gaulle's return was essential to a solution of the Algerian crisis.[4] By the end of 1957 the possibility of de Gaulle's return being widely and favourably discussed by senior members of the civilian and military bureaucracies in Paris.[5] Opinion polls revealed a parallel trend: at the end of 1955 only one per cent of respondents favoured a de Gaulle-led government; in April 1956 five per cent; in July 1956 nine per cent; in September 1957 eleven per cent; and in January 1958 thirteen per cent.[6] On the other hand, thirteen per cent hardly constituted the tidal wave of popular support that de Gaulle was looking for. And Coty's opinion – crucial as it was in the dénouement of the May 1958 crisis – was certainly not shared by the political class as a whole. On the eve of the crisis, most politicians, political commentators, and – so far as we can tell – citizens remained sceptical that the sixty-seven year old General would ever play a major role in politics again.[7]

All that changed when the Fourth Republic entered its final agony. On 8 February 1958, French planes attacked an FLN base in Tunisia and inadvertently destroyed the adjacent village of Sakhiet. The large number of civilian deaths in Sakhiet provoked an international outcry. In the aftermath, the French government, headed at the time by Félix Gaillard, bowed to foreign pressure and agreed to accept American and British mediation over the incident. This 'capitulation' was denounced in Algeria as well as by Gaullist and nationalist politicians in Paris. On 15 April the government lost a confidence vote in parliament and Gaillard resigned.

Even before mid-April, the Sakhiet incident and its

sequel had crystallized long-standing hostilities towards the republic, both on the part of the army in Algeria, which felt that it was close to achieving military victory and was all the more exasperated by the weakness of the civilian authorities, and on the part of the settler population. By March 1958 an array of groups mobilizing *pieds noirs*, army officers, right-wing politicians, and a few committed Gaullists were actively plotting insurrection against the Fourth Republic. Some of these groups envisaged the return of General de Gaulle in the wake of the insurrection, though many did not (the *pieds noirs* had generally been Pétainist during the war and many officers either viewed de Gaulle as over the hill or still resented his indiscipline in 1940). De Gaulle himself was far from fully informed about the detail of these plots, but he was aware of their existence, having been sounded out by people involved in them.[8] He was also aware of various machinations on his behalf in Paris. In early 1958 he received a stream of well-placed visitors during his fortnightly trips to the capital. Through his aides, particularly Jacques Foccart and Olivier Guichard, he was kept informed of rumours and developments in the French political world.

By early May, this world was in the final stages of disintegration. A series of attempts to form a new coalition government had failed, and on 5 May President Coty sent a message to de Gaulle, asking whether he would be willing to enter into negotiations to form a government. At that point, before any actual emergency had occurred in Algeria and before Coty or any other political leader had made a public appeal to him, de Gaulle declined. His main concern was not to act prematurely. As he knew, the momentum was still building in his favour. Rumours of impending action in Algiers filtered back to him, and on 11 May the editor of a leading Algiers newspaper published the first public appeal for his return. Two days later, on 13 May, shortly before a Christian democrat by the name of Pierre Pflimlin made yet another attempt – as it turned out, successful – to win a vote of confidence in the National Assembly in Paris, a crowd took over the main government building in Algiers. The rebellion had begun.

Initially, the crowd's actions took many of the insurrectionists (including the Gaullists) by surprise. Over the next few hours, however, the latter were able to regain control of the situation and turn it to their advantage. A Committee of Public Safety was hastily constituted. The military commander of the city of Algiers, General Massu, who was also one of the few fervent Gaullists among the senior officers, agreed to head this committee. Just before midnight on 13 May, Massu read the following statement from the balcony of the government building: 'We appeal to General de Gaulle, the only man who is capable of heading a Government of Public Safety, above all the parties, in order to ensure the perpetuation of French Algeria as an integral part of France.'9 In Paris, the government's response was an admission of impotence: it turned civilian authority over to the Commander-in-Chief, General Raoul Salan.

De Gaulle recognized that the crisis that he had been anticipating since 1946 had finally arrived. But still he did not break his silence. No doubt, he wished to avoid any impression that he was working in coordination with the insurrection in Algiers or responding to the summons of the committee. It was not until 15 May, when General Salan gave an official stamp to Massu's appeal by concluding a speech with the words 'Vive de Gaulle', that the General spoke. He issued a terse statement to the press, indicating that he was 'ready to assume the powers of the Republic'. Four days later, on 19 May, he held his first press conference since June 1955 and elaborated on the two main points of his earlier statement: first, he stressed his personal legitimacy based on his exploits between 1940 and 1946; second, he declared his readiness to be 'useful again to France'. Notably absent from his remarks were any clear or explicit indications of the terms on which he would agree to return or any clear or explicit criticism of the insurrection in Algiers. Reading between the lines, it was evident that de Gaulle was seeking to encourage those individuals in the political establishment – such as President Coty and the deputy prime minister, Guy Mollet – who were already moving towards a Gaullist solution, but that he was not yet willing to negotiate with the collective leadership of the Republic. He still needed to encourage supporters in the army and in the civilian population to keep up their pressure on the regime. This attitude was bitterly criticized by republican politicians who felt that he had given an enormous fillip to a rebellion that would otherwise have run out of steam.[10]

The politicians' disapproval would have been sharper still had they been aware of plans already taking shape in the army to launch an actual invasion of mainland France if the regime refused to recall de Gaulle to power. Operation Resurrection, as it was called, was first mooted in the immediate aftermath of 13 May. As early as 18 May, one of the leading Gaullist conspirators, Michel Debré, was informed by a high-ranking officer that the operation was ready for launching whenever the General gave the signal that his return to power 'by legal means' had been blocked. However, the officer also warned that the army's deadline was the end of the month and that, if de Gaulle did not respond to its appeal, the army would go ahead with Operation Resurrection nonetheless.[11]

Over the next ten days de Gaulle played a very dangerous and difficult game, in which he manipulated the threat of Operation Resurrection without overtly backing or overtly disavowing the army's plans. When he sensed that the politicians were afraid enough of the army to come to terms with him (as they seemed to be after learning that troops based in Algeria had seized control of the island of Corsica on 24–25 May), he flashed a red light to Algiers and moved on the political front in Paris. On 26 May he wrote to Mollet and to Prime Minister Pflimlin, proposing face-to-face meetings. On 27 May, after a private meeting with Pflimlin, he issued a communiqué declaring that he had begun 'the proper process necessary for the establishment of a republican government', and urging the troops in Algeria to remain 'exemplary, under the command of their leaders'. However, it was certainly not Pflimlin's understanding that his meeting with de Gaulle had begun the process of forming a new government. A majority of the deputies in parliament rallied to support Pflimlin and reject what they interpreted as de Gaulle's scarcely concealed blackmail. At that point, the General apparently cancelled the red light to Algiers. On 28 May, he had a meeting with General Dulac, who had come to Colombey as an emissary from General Salan, to brief him about plans for Operation Resurrection. If Dulac's version of the interview is to be believed, de Gaulle acknowledged the possibility that he might have to come to power after a military operation against Paris. 'It would have been immensely preferable for my return to be accomplished by the [legal] process,' de Gaulle told Dulac, but added cryptically: 'Tell General Salan that what he has done and what he will do is for the good of France.'[12]

This interview was one of several direct or indirect communications between de Gaulle and leaders of Operation Resurrection which have been the subject of intense controversy. The issue they raise is charged with the heaviest moral and political overtones: did de Gaulle at any point give the go-ahead for Operation Resurrection? If one understands by this an explicit order to launch an invasion, the answer would appear to be no. On the other hand, de Gaulle undoubtedly knew about the invasion plan, did not declare unambiguously against it (because he needed it to be a plausible threat in order to coerce the republican leadership), and, when the regime's resistance stiffened momentarily on 27–28 May, was willing to contemplate coming to power as a result of it. By most criteria, this behaviour would constitute a form of complicity.

To understand why he was willing to take such an immense risk with his own reputation as well as with France's future, one must look beyond personal ambition. The critical factor was the depth of his contempt for the Fourth Republic. Quite simply, he placed a higher priority on removing the existing regime than on forestalling a military intervention. For him, the worst possible outcome was not the one feared by republicans and dutifully recorded in his memoirs – a coup followed by a protracted civil war between the army and a communist-led Popular Front. Worse still would have been for the republic to wriggle out of its predicament, most likely by appointing de Gaulle as an emergency premier so as to appease the army. In that event, de Gaulle's prestige would have been expended without any lasting benefit. Once things had returned to normal, he would have been quietly elbowed out of power so that the parties could resume their disastrous 'game'. De Gaulle had already experienced a variation on this theme in 1945–46. In May 1958, he showed his determination to avoid a recurrence.

De Gaulle conducted his strategy with consummate skill.

He did not move prematurely. He gave enough encourage-
ment to the army command without losing control of the
situation altogether. His public pronouncements and
statements were brilliantly timed and phrased to send the
right signals to Algiers, raise popular expectations at home,
and undermine the credibility of the Pflimlin government.
Once the regime began to crumble, he made a number of
pro forma but symbolically important concessions to
appease republican sensibilities and to brush up his
republican image, which had been tarnished by the RPF
adventure.

For all his skill, however, it is essential to realize that the
strategy might very well have failed, but for the intervention of President Coty. When Pflimlin resigned (on
28 May), Coty took the initiative of inviting de Gaulle to
form a government and threatening parliament with his
own resignation if it denied de Gaulle. This proved a turning-
point. On 31 May de Gaulle formed his cabinet and on 1
June presented it to the National Assembly, where it was
confirmed by the margin of 329 votes to 224 (with the
majority composed of conservatives, centrists, and half the
socialist deputies). He was then granted full power for six
months as well as authority to draw up a new constitution,
which would be put to a popular referendum for ratifica-
tion. In the end de Gaulle's strategy had succeeded, but
the fact that it had required Coty's intervention to be
successful showed just how risky it had been.

. . .

De Gaulle's priorities on becoming the Fourth Republic's
last prime minister had a familiar ring to anybody who remembered his actions in the 1940s. His first priority was to
restore national unity by closing the breach between
France and France-in-Algeria and rallying the nation
around the person of General de Gaulle. As in 1944 he
formed a government which symbolized unity: each of the
main parties (this time excluding the PCF) was allotted
three ministries. He then used his personal popularity and
legitimacy to win public support for his regime. He made a
series of trips to Algeria reminiscent of those that he had
made to the French provinces in the autumn of 1944. The
first and most dramatic, in early June, set the tone for the

rest. In the Forum in Algiers de Gaulle told a huge crowd of settlers and Muslims: 'Je vous ai compris!' ('I have understood you!') His aim in this and other speeches was not to indicate his solution to the crisis (although that was often how his words were heard) but to make an emotional connection with each of the major parties to the conflict (the settlers, the Muslims, and the army) as well as with the population at home. Until new institutions could be put in place, this common confidence in de Gaulle was the only effective source of unity in the nation.

A second priority was to restore order, especially in Algeria. This required two steps: the reimposition of state control over insurrectionist authorities such as the Committees of Public Safety; and the restoration of a clear distinction between military and civilian spheres. This distinction had been blurred not only by officers' participation in the committees but by the Pflimlin government's delegation of supreme civilian authority to the Commander-in-Chief, General Salan. De Gaulle handled the problem of the committees in much the same way that he had dealt with resistance organizations in 1944. He moved quickly to cut short any illusions that they might have about possessing an independent authority or having de Gaulle in their debt. He told Salan to deny them official status and to limit strictly their interference in public affairs.[13] On the other hand, until he was firmly in charge, de Gaulle avoided an open confrontation with them. Instead, he preferred to let them fade into irrelevance until he was ready to deliver the *coup de grâce*, which came in October, when he ordered all military personnel to withdraw from them.

The army itself was handled with considerably more caution. Having offended officers by omitting Jacques Soustelle, the most well-known Gaullist advocate of French Algeria, from his first government, de Gaulle appeased them by bringing Soustelle into the government in July. He also allowed Salan to remain in sole possession of military and civilian authority, and treated him with ostentatious respect and cordiality. In fact, he intended all along to replace Salan and restore the civil–military distinction, but it was not until the referendum had approved his new constitution that he notified Salan of his intentions.

For all the tact of his dealings with the army, his words

and policies in the summer of 1958 plainly showed that de Gaulle was disassociating himself from the ideology of integration – i.e. integration of Algeria into France – that many officers favoured. His reluctance to use the slogan of 'French Algeria' (apart from on one occasion at the end of his first trip) was certainly not lost on the integrationists, who were grumbling by July.[14] Instead of stressing the Frenchness of all Algerians, de Gaulle's speeches stressed the equality of all citizens in Algeria, which could either mean the same thing or something quite different. On 4 June he announced that in the forthcoming referendum and elections Algeria would have a single electoral college, rather than the old dual college system, which had guaranteed an over-representation for Europeans. He also made it clear that in his view a lasting political settlement could only be achieved when the Algerian people made their wishes known through the ballot box.[15] This emphasis on political equality could be interpreted as a snub to the forces of violence (the FLN), but since there were more than eight million Muslims and only one million Europeans it was hardly comforting to proponents of integration. Even less comforting were the implications of a plan for the progressive decolonization of the French empire that de Gaulle unveiled in the summer of 1958. De Gaulle's proposals for a 'French Community' included a provision that any colony which wished to break all ties with France would be free to do so, simply by voting no in the constitutional referendum. Algeria was not, strictly speaking, a colony, but the implications of this recognition of the independence option were unmistakeable.[16]

These various statements amounted to straws in the wind rather than a fully defined policy for ending the war. The evolution of de Gaulle's Algerian policy will be discussed in the next chapter, but at this point it should be noted that until the summer of 1959 the policy was essentially a holding operation. De Gaulle made limited overtures to all sides – offering the FLN an honourable truce ('paix des braves') but refusing to negotiate with it as a political force; throwing some rhetorical sops to the integrationists but refusing to embrace the cause of integration; telling the army that outright victory should be its objective, but also saying that no resolution reached against the will of the Algerian people would endure for long. Some have argued that this policy of ambiguity and delay reflected wishful thinking on his part, a misguided belief that he could somehow parlay his personal standing with all parties into a new consensus that would hold the communities together long enough for a French-financed modernization programme to work its magic. Others have interpreted it as tactical manoeuvring, a manifestation of his habitual tendency to have two or more irons in the fire. Certainly, he had to face the fact that a majority of the French population still supported the principle of integration[17] and that there were immense risks involved in challenging integration head-on, especially since the malaise in the army was still a factor to be reckoned with.[18] He may also have felt that the time was not ripe for any definitive initiative. That is the implication of a very suggestive comment that he made at the time to Edgar Faure: 'At certain periods there are some problems that have no solution.'[19] Rather than attempt a premature resolution, de Gaulle preferred to take care of first things first, that is to renovate the state in Paris. When the time came to act in Algeria, he could then do so from a position of strength rather than weakness.

De Gaulle's third priority in 1958 was to use the authority that he had been granted by parliament in early June to undertake the essential work of renewal. The urgency and decisiveness with which he moved over the following six months contrasted markedly with his tentative performance in the post-liberation period and obviously reflected the hard lessons that he had learned. Within a matter of weeks he had put in place a constituent procedure entirely different from the parliamentary procedure of 1945–46. The constitution of the Fifth Republic was prepared in two committees – one chaired by de Gaulle and including senior ministers and members of de Gaulle's entourage, the other chaired by the Minister of Justice, Debré, and composed of experts from the Conseil d'Etat. After the draft had been reviewed by a Consultative Constitutional Committee – the only stage at which parliamentarians had an opportunity to present their views – it was submitted directly to the people for approval in a referendum. All participants agree that Debré was the main architect of the constitution, but de Gaulle played an active supervisory role, intervening not just to ensure conformity with Bayeux principles but often to insist on specific wording or specific clauses (such as the article which gave the president the right to assume full powers in the event of a national emergency).[20]

The new constitution was a hybrid of presidential and parliamentary systems. Technically, it was not a presidential system, because it provided for a dual executive, with a president and a prime minister. The latter was chosen by the president but could be removed by a parliamentary vote of censure (thus confirming the republican principle of executive accountability to the legislature). In practice, however, the new republic's distinguishing feature, in marked contrast to either the Third or the Fourth Republic, was the enormous power of the president. The change was symbolized in the order of the clauses, which broke all republican precedents by placing those dealing with the president before those dealing with parliament. It was reflected in the four great powers that the constitution gave the president: to appoint and accept the resignation of the prime minister (which in practice also came to mean dismiss the prime minister); to dissolve the National Assembly; to submit important constitutional issues to a popular referendum; and to exercise supreme power in a national crisis.[21] Critics charged that the president was a 'veritable monarch'.[22] Privately, de Gaulle agreed.[23] Publicly, he defended the president's huge powers as imperative for national survival in the late-twentieth century. At Bayeux in 1946 he had quoted the ancient Greek lawmaker Solon, who was asked to name the best constitution and replied: 'Tell me first for which people and in which era.' Presenting his constitution at a huge outdoor rally in Paris on 4 September 1958, de Gaulle echoed this advice. He explained that since France was living in a period of rapid economic, technological, political, and diplomatic change, she needed a government which could provide sustained and effective leadership.

The distinctive feature of de Gaulle's constitutional ideology was its combination of this kind of modernizing vision with an unshakeable belief in his personal destiny. In 1958 he believed that he was founding a republic that would serve France well for many years to come, but he also believed that in the immediate future his presence was essential to France's safety and renewal. Superimposed on the abstract relationships of the constitution was a living relationship between de Gaulle and France. Ultimately, it was the latter which guided de Gaulle's actions, and when the two came into conflict (as they did in 1962, over the issue of constitutional revision) it was the abstract relationship that had to yield.

. . .

While he was supervising the preparation of his constitution and orchestrating its presentation to the people of France and the French Community, de Gaulle moved decisively on a number of other fronts, particularly economic and diplomatic. The diplomatic initiatives of 1958 will be discussed in later chapters, since they were plainly envisaged as the first steps in a long-term strategy. More immediate preoccupations were the domestic economic problems (inflation, budget deficits, and trade deficits) which had long eroded the Fourth Republic's popularity, not to mention French national self-esteem. De Gaulle used the extraordinary powers granted to him in June to introduce a set of major economic measures, which were intended to remedy these problems and to show France and the world that a state worthy of the name was now in charge.

The origins of the ambitious economic reform of 1958 lay in the weeks immediately after de Gaulle's return. In June, one of France's leading economic experts, Jacques Rueff, approached the new minister of finance, Antoine Pinay, with a proposal for a sweeping 'programme of economic and financial renovation'.[24] Rueff's initiative was rather reminiscent of Monnet's in 1945: in both cases, de Gaulle's reputation as a decisive policy-maker sympathetic to modernization encouraged a person with ambitious ideas to come forward. Pinay was at first reluctant to pursue the project, which in all probability would have died an administrative death, had de Gaulle not let off a series of explosions of impatience with the footdragging of the Finance Ministry.[25] Prodded by de Gaulle, Pinay created a secret committee, chaired by Rueff, which worked quickly to draw up a plan. The Rueff plan, which was presented to de Gaulle in mid-November, had three main planks: a substantial devaluation of the franc (accompanied by the creation of a new franc equivalent to 100 old francs); action to control the budget deficit, both through increased taxes and cuts in governmental expenditure; and a decision to remove many restrictions on foreign trade and to reduce tariffs on trade with the other five Common Market countries (in line with a commitment that had been made by the Fourth Republic the year before). In the long term, this final measure was the most momentous of all. When the Treaties of Rome creating the Common Market and Euratom had been signed in 1957, de Gaulle had criticized them and told aides that, if he came back to power, he would 'destroy' them. His change of heart may well have been motivated more by politics than economics – it has been suggested that the British government's persistent efforts to block the Market were enough to convince de Gaulle of its virtues – but the economic implications of allowing the Common Market to take effect on schedule were profound.[26] France's entry into the Market was a crucial factor in sustaining the growth and modernization of the French economy in the years ahead.

At the time Rueff's proposals were, to put it mildly, unpopular. Pinay himself opposed them, as did most of the other ministers.[27] The Bank of France and business leaders opposed them. When they were announced, opinion polls indicated strong opposition from the public.[28] Unlike thirteen years earlier, however, de Gaulle was not in the least deterred by warnings of dire consequences. He overrode his finance minister's objections and at the crucial cabinet meeting threatened his own resignation if his ministers did not approve the plan.[29] He backed it not just because he was convinced by Rueff and his advisers that it would reduce inflation and revitalize the economy through the stimulus of competition, but because he was attracted by its theatrical elements – the symbolism of a new franc to mark a new political order, the grand gesture of carrying out commitments to Europe that the Fourth Republic had given up hopes of honouring, the rhetoric of a coherent plan of renovation as opposed to a collection of policies. De Gaulle's faith in the value of the plan was amply justified by what followed: not only a substantial improvement in such indices as gold and currency reserves, balance of trade, and inflation, but a transformation in perceptions of the economy, inside France but especially abroad. Suddenly, the economic miracle of the past decade began to be recognized for what it was. One observer spoke of 'la panique de la confiance'.[30]

Indeed, that expression would be apt for the year 1958 as a whole. At the beginning of the year, the mood of the nation had been pessimistic: trapped in a tragic war, to which increasingly there seemed no happy outcome, oppressed by a fear of national decline and stagnation, not so much hostile to the regime as indifferent to it. In May, with the sudden spectre of civil war, pessimism turned to panic. Certainly de Gaulle could not have returned to power if he had not stepped forward and risked a great deal in the process. Nor could he have returned to power without the machinations of devoted supporters who worked to foment unrest in Algeria and then to channel it in his favour. For all that, the key to his return was the total panic of May and the total lack of confidence in the capacity of the existing regime to extricate France from the crisis. There was a vacuum waiting to be filled. This explains the curious fact that so few people expected de Gaulle to return before May, but, once he had returned, so many placed their confidence in him. The panic of despair became, almost instantaneously, the panic of confidence.

This confidence was given a democratic sanction in the referendum of 28 September 1958. Seventy-nine per cent of metropolitan French voters approved the new republic. Voters in Algeria and in twelve out of thirteen member states in the Community also gave de Gaulle resounding votes of confidence. Two months later, at the end of November, legislative elections swept most of the old republic's parliamentary elite out of office. A new Gaullist party, the Union pour la Nouvelle République (UNR – Union for the New Republic), became the largest single party, in spite of the fact that de Gaulle carefully maintained his distance from it and did not play any role in the election campaign. The Communist Party, which had campaigned against the new constitution, saw its parliamentary representation decimated, while the non-communist left, which had been split on the constitution, lost half of its seats. On 21 December, de Gaulle was elected as the first

President of the Fifth Republic, with 78.5 per cent of the votes cast by an electoral college of 80,000 'notables'. On 8 January 1959 he was officially inaugurated and two days later formed the first government of the new republic, headed by Michel Debré.

Walking back to his office after the ceremony in January 1959, de Gaulle is reported to have turned to his new prime minister and said: 'This evening I will return to Colombey. You will take over from me.' When Debré protested that the people would not understand his departure, de Gaulle replied: 'I will not be able to do what I want to do, it is too late . . .'[31] This peculiar outburst was entirely in character for de Gaulle, who could be serenely optimistic in the heat of a crisis only to become sceptical and disillusioned, even depressed, when the crisis was over. Perhaps, as Debré suggests, he realized that he had now become a prisoner of his own institutions, President de Gaulle instead of General de Gaulle. Perhaps, as he himself later suggested in his memoirs, he was assailed by a sense of living and leading in a less heroic era than that of the 1940s.[32] Or perhaps he had a premonition of the huge effort that lay ahead if he was to extricate France from a crisis in Algeria that had reached the verge of insolubility.

. . .

NOTES AND REFERENCES

1. De Gaulle C 1970 *Mémoires d'espoir* (2 vols). Plon, Paris, vol. 1 pp. 22–3.
2. Smith T 1978 *The French Stake in Algeria, 1945–1962*. Cornell UP, Ithaca, pp. 22–8.
3. Rioux J-P 1983 *La France de la Quatrième République* (2 vols). Le Seuil, Paris, vol. 2 pp. 145–8.
4. Rudelle O 1988 *Mai 58: De Gaulle et la République*. Plon, Paris, p. 81.
5. Rudelle O 1988 p. 91.
6. Charlot J 1971 *The Gaullist Phenomenon* trans M Charlot, M Neighbour. Allen and Unwin, p. 45.
7. Rémond R 1983 *Le Retour de de Gaulle*. Editions Complexe, Brussels, p. 58.
8. Rudelle O 1988 pp. 107–10.
9. Massu J 1972 *Le Torrent et la digue*. Plon, Paris, p. 52.
10. Mendès-France P 1987 *Oeuvres complètes* (6 vols). Gallimard, Paris, vol. 4 pp. 412–14.

11. Debré M 1988 *Mémoires* (3 vols). Albin Michel, Paris, vol. 2 pp. 307–8.
12. Rudelle O 1988 p. 248.
13. Letters of 6/6/58, 21/6/58, 22/7/58, LNC vol. 8 pp. 21, 35, 52.
14. Tricot B 1972 *Les Sentiers de la paix. Algérie 1958–1962.* Plon, Paris, p. 37.
15. Speech of 27/6/58, DM vol. 3 pp. 19–20.
16. Daniel J 1986 *De Gaulle et l'Algérie.* Le Seuil, Paris, pp. 25, 69.
17. Droz B, Lever E 1982 *Histoire de la guerre d'Algérie.* Le Seuil, Paris, p. 194.
18. Daniel J 1986 pp. 107–8.
19. Lacouture J 1986 *De Gaulle* (3 vols). Le Seuil, Paris, vol. 3 p. 50.
20. Debré M 1988 vol. 2 pp. 376–7.
21. Chapsal J 1981 *La Vie politique sous la Ve République.* PUF, Paris, pp. 99–110.
22. Mendès-France P 1987 vol. 4 p. 438.
23. Letter of 4/6/61, LNC vol. 9 p. 94.
24. Rueff J 1977 *De l'aube au crépuscule.* Plon, Paris, pp. 228–9.
25. 1986 *1958: la faillite ou le miracle.* Economica, Paris, pp. 49–50.
26. Lacouture J 1985 *De Gaulle* (3 vols). Le Seuil, Paris, vol. 2 pp. 629–30, 645.
27. 1986 *1958: la faillite ou le miracle* pp. 62–3.
28. Guillaume S 1984 *Antoine Pinay ou la confiance en politique.* FNSP, Paris, p. 183.
29. Lacouture J 1985 vol. 2 p. 676.
30. André Maurois, quoted in *1958, la faillite ou le miracle* p. 75.
31. Debré M 1988 vol. 3 pp. 17–18.
32. De Gaulle C 1970 vol. 1 pp. 39–40.

Chapter 6

1959–62: ALGERIA AND BEYOND

The first three years of de Gaulle's presidency were dominated by the Algerian war. Ending this conflict was his
main, at times his sole, preoccupation. It proved to be a
long, painful, and frustrating operation, which along the
way provoked two serious insurrections against the regime,
alienated much of the army, and left behind lifelong
resentments. In the end, de Gaulle could only secure peace
at the expense of a series of humiliating concessions to the
FLN – concessions which could be justified only on the
grounds that they averted the yet higher costs of not
making them. To use a popular metaphor from the time,
getting out of Algeria was like paying off the mortgage on
the nation's future.

This was certainly not the most glamorous or heroic of
episodes. Perhaps that was why de Gaulle's memoirs of the
period, *Memoirs of Hope*, de-dramatized the whole affair, re-
ducing it to a futile conflict over the essentially nineteenth-
century problem of colonial domination, irrelevant to the
real concerns of France in the contemporary era. Largely
missing from de Gaulle's account were the dilemmas, ambi-
guities, illusions, deceptions, and self-deceptions that gave
these years their poignancy. The irony is that in striving to
perpetuate a certain mythology about his own prescience
and consistency, about France's fundamental unity, and
about the mediocrity of the times in comparison with the
exalted hours of the war and the liberation, de Gaulle
actually masked one of the great achievements, perhaps the
greatest achievement, of his political career.[1] For even if
the setting did not have the same grandeur and the

leading characters did not have the same epic cast as twenty years earlier, the role that de Gaulle himself had to play was at least as arduous as that which he had played in the Second World War.

To appreciate the extent of his achievement in extricating France from Algeria, one must recognize what he preferred to play down in his memoirs, namely the colossal constraints under which he operated. All the structural realities of the situation there made for an impasse. The army was determined not to repeat its humiliating retreat from Indochina. The settlers were determined to retain their privileged status. The FLN was determined to continue the war, as were the FLN's backers in other countries. Any policy which sought reconciliation with one or more of these forces was, *ipso facto*, bound to offend one or more others. In addition, a majority of de Gaulle's own political supporters, including his prime minister Debré, believed fervently that Algeria should remain part of France. Even when he could overcome their resistance, he could not trust his military and civilian bureaucracies to put his policies into operation in the manner that he desired. More often than not, the transmission of his directives across the Mediterranean was an occasion for their systematic 'reinterpretation' by officials committed to the cause of French Algeria.

In order to overcome these constraints, de Gaulle had to rely chiefly upon himself – upon the powers which he held as president, but more importantly upon the prestige of his name and the authority of his voice. France's Algerian policy was his policy, not only in the sense that he made the critical decisions about when and how to launch an initiative or offer a concession, but because he personified the policy. Between June 1958 and December 1960 he made eight trips to Algeria. On other occasions he communicated with the people of Algeria and the army via radio and television broadcasts. In all these encounters, direct or indirect, he never once hesitated to draw on the capital of his own history. When he urged the *pieds noirs* to give up integration, when he ordered the army to remain loyal, when he appealed to the FLN to lay down their arms and negotiate, he evoked not just the powers and responsibilities of his office but the confidence that they should have in the person of himself, General de Gaulle. One of the hard lessons of this crisis was that there were limits to the power of his charisma and prestige, especially with people in Algeria. By and large, however, he did retain the confidence of the French people, whose attitude towards the war developed in line with the evolution of his policy. Ultimately, this popular support proved to be his greatest resource.

. . .

As we have seen, de Gaulle's initial policies in Algeria appeared contradictory. Did this in some degree reflect contradictions in de Gaulle's own thinking? In his memoirs, which are monuments to his own consistency, he answered this question in the negative: while admitting that he had no pre-established plan (naturally since that would have been the kind of dogmatic thinking that he abhorred), he insisted that 'the broad outlines were fixed in my mind . . . [T]here was no longer, in my view, any solution except to give Algeria the right to self-determination.'[2] On balance historians have tended to accept this retrospective view. They have turned up numerous occasions before June 1958 when de Gaulle expressed either scepticism about forced integration or a belief in self-determination. For example, that was the view that he had expressed to his old wartime comrade Maurice Schumann in February 1958.[3] A month later a high-ranking army officer had heard him deliver the following verdict on integration: 'They are not Provençals or Languedocians. They are Arabs and they will never be integrated.'[4]

This did not necessarily mean that de Gaulle already took for granted that self-determination would lead to an independent Algerian state. He had certainly mentioned the possibility of independence as far back as the mid-1950s.[5] But to take such comments as proof that de Gaulle already knew what he would have to do in 1962 is a leap made only by Gaullists predisposed to elevate the General's prescience to superhuman levels or by fanatical anti-Gaullists predisposed to exaggerate the depths of his duplicity. A more plausible interpretation, both less prescient and less duplicitous, would suggest that, while de Gaulle recognized the possibility of independence – and one might well wonder how, in the midst of global decolonization, he could have avoided such a recognition – he was by no means certain that this was the only possible outcome in Algeria. His early predictions of independence should probably not be taken as settled opinions but rather as conversational ploys: he often tried out extreme views on his audience, to test their reactions or to play out scenarios in his own mind. Independence was not the only such scenario that he had mentioned. As early as 1955, for example, he had floated the idea of a new 'association' between Algeria and France.[6]

Once he was in power, this alternative view would argue, his policies were more consistent with a belief that it was still feasible to salvage some kind of organic link between France and Algeria than with a belief in the inevitability of complete rupture. It is suggestive that his initial conception of the French Community (which he subsequently modified to meet the objections of black African leaders) would have denied African nations the option of independence.[7] If he did not initially envisage independence for black Africa, it is difficult to believe that he did envisage it for the *départements* of French Algeria. In fact, in so far as one can detect a firm line in his early Algerian policy, it was a policy which aimed to achieve association – i.e. cooperation between France and a more autonomous but not fully independent Algeria. While pursuing a short-term strategy that combined military campaigns against the FLN with political overtures to the Algerian masses, de Gaulle launched an ambitious long-term policy to make such an association possible. At Constantine, on 3 October 1958, he proposed a far-reaching five-year plan to modernize Algerian agriculture and industry, improve housing, education, and public works, and open up careers and jobs to Muslims. The aims of this plan were to produce a new generation of francophile elites and to convince Algerians that only France was willing and able to modernize their country.

Historians are divided on how seriously to take this association idea. Did de Gaulle really believe in it? When did he cease basing his policy on it? The answer to the second question, as we shall see, is probably late 1960 or early 1961. The first question is more difficult to answer.

One problem is the vagueness of the whole concept. At the outset, it seemed to mean a structure (like the initial form of the French Community) which would allow France to retain control over significant areas of policy-making. Later on, it seemed to signify a much looser framework in which France would receive certain minimal concessions in return for economic aid. This vagueness was inherent in a concept which expressed deep-rooted instincts rather than a carefully conceived policy. When he talked about the 'transformation' of Algeria, as he did a great deal in 1959 and 1960, de Gaulle slipped back into the rhetoric of his other association idea (labour-capital association), a rhetoric which was influenced by the social catholicism of his early years. It was the same idealistic but essentially woolly vision of institutionalized divisions melting away as human contacts and common interests developed between the two entrenched camps. The attraction of the concept was that it allowed him to square a number of circles at once. He could accept self-determination and advance the prospects of a political settlement without burning his boats with the army – to whom he presented association as the first step towards a real, consensual integration[8] – and without seeming to capitulate or feeling that he was capitulating to the FLN.

The essential flaw in association, as a practical strategy, was that it could only work – i.e. neutralize the FLN and end the war – in the long term. It did nothing about the immediate problems, and so, probably inevitably, came to be seen as a form of inaction. During the first months of his presidency, the pressure to adopt a more aggressive policy mounted. This pressure came from all sides – from outside France (from the United Nations and the US, in particular); from public opinion at home, which was showing a growing disenchantment with the war; from advisers who argued that, for all the army's military successes, the prospects of outright victory were distant and the FLN had little or no incentive to stop fighting;[9] and, last but not least, from his own impatience. His constitution was now in place, his political position at home was very strong, but he was almost seventy years of age and could hardly afford to sit back and wait for a long-term transformation to solve Algeria's problems.

So, in the summer of 1959, without abandoning association,

de Gaulle decided to force the pace of his policy. At the end of August he consulted with his ministers and then with his senior commanders in Algeria. He also alerted the leaders of the FLN and President Eisenhower to a new initiative. After laying the groundwork, he announced this initiative in a broadcast address from the Elysée Palace on 16 September 1959. This 'self-determination' speech, as it became known, was probably the most important that he delivered during the Algerian conflict – not because it expressed radically new ideas, but because it expressed openly and in concrete terms what had hitherto been implicit. De Gaulle pledged that, within four years of a ceasefire, the Algerian people would be consulted democratically about their future. He told them that they would have three options. The first was total independence, which de Gaulle called, derogatorily, 'secession'. The second was total integration, which, equally derogatorily, he called 'francisation'. The third was unnamed, but it was clearly association – 'government of Algerians by Algerians, supported by French aid and in close union with France'.

The speech provides a perfect example of the way de Gaulle used language, not just to express opinions but to shape a fluid situation. It served a number of different purposes. On one level, it sought to frame the public debate (why only three options? why not four or five?) in such a way as to create a consensus around his policy. The two radical solutions were described in such extreme terms that the middle ground was made to seem huge and inviting, far larger than it actually was. On another level, de Gaulle's public recognition of self-determination and the option of independence opened up new possibilities for negotiation. This was an opening not just to the FLN, from whom de Gaulle hoped (unsuccessfully, as it transpired) to force a response, but to the Algerian people as a whole. On yet another level, however, de Gaulle provided just enough mystery about his own preferences to allow those who wanted to believe in 'francisation' to go on believing that he shared their views.[10] He encouraged such self-deception. In the interest of minimizing opposition to his initiative, he allowed rumours to circulate in army circles to the effect that the speech had been aimed primarily at the UN which was about to debate the war.[11]

In spite of this precaution, the speech came as a great shock to most of the officers in Algeria, indeed to the army as a whole. Its implications for the war they were fighting were profoundly unsettling: even in the best case – from their perspective, 'francisation' – they would still be in the position of fighting against an independence movement in the name of self-determination. This made little or no sense to them. And for a small minority of colonels, the speech represented a final proof that de Gaulle had betrayed the cause of French Algeria once and for all. They now began to side with the extreme wing of the *pied noir* integrationist movement, which openly called for his overthrow.

And yet de Gaulle himself was remarkably confident that the army would toe the line. In spite of being informed about the widespread criticism of his speech, he confided to his aide-de-camp that 'the army can do nothing against me'.[12] As for the *pieds noirs*, his attitude was tinged with more than a little contempt: he did not think that 'southern types' like them could threaten his regime.[13] Four months after the self-determination speech he received a rude awakening on both scores. The discontent with de Gaulle's policies, which had been building steadily since 1958, suddenly burst into the open.

The events of what came to be known as Barricades Week began on 18 January 1960, when a German newspaper published an interview with General Massu, in which he openly attacked de Gaulle's self-determination policy. De Gaulle was incensed, ordered Massu's recall to Paris, and, against the advice of several senior advisers, insisted that Massu should not be permitted to return to his command. When de Gaulle was warned that the recall of a soldier who was so popular with the *pieds noirs* might spark disturbances in Algeria, his reply was adamant: 'If this decision provokes some local unrest, well we shall see. This unrest, under the circumstances, can only be limited and circumstantial. But the humiliation of the state and de Gaulle's consenting to it would be irreparable.'[14]

The backlash was more violent than de Gaulle expected. On 24 January, when Algiers learned of Massu's fate, a general strike was called and barricades were erected in the streets. There were a number of bloody incidents, and then a standoff, during which elements of the army fraternized with the insurrectionists. The days which followed were among the most difficult in de Gaulle's entire presidency. Algiers was in open rebellion. When the prime minister, Michel Debré, made a dramatic trip there, he was verbally accosted by dissident officers who demanded that the government reverse its policy of self-determination. Even some members of de Gaulle's own staff at the Elysée were apparently sympathetic to the insurrection.

De Gaulle himself was shocked by the events and at first hesitant about what to do. He talked about using force but knew that such a step might provoke a greater crisis or might even break the loyalty of his army. In the end, he had two trump cards to play. The first was the support of a large majority of the French public, not just for him personally but for his policy of self-determination. The second was his unrivalled ability to project his authority to Algeria and to the army. On 29 January, wearing a military uniform to show that he was General de Gaulle as well as President de Gaulle, he spoke to the nation on radio and television. His speech pulled out all the stops. He resolutely defended the policy of self-determination. He appealed directly to the *pieds noirs* and the army, using rhetoric that combined intimidating references to the authority of the state with tendentious but effective arguments to reassure them about the 'real' aim of his policy. He concluded with an emotionally charged and lyrical appeal to France: 'Well, my dear old country, here we are together, once again, facing a harsh test.' All observers agreed that the effect on the situation in Algiers was profound. The following day, with the barricades still in place but support for the insurrection eroding, de Gaulle was already talking about the crisis in the past tense. The day after that, the leaders of the insurrection surrendered.

Barricades Week showed just how far de Gaulle still was from being able to end the Algerian crisis. At the same time, having in the end faced down the rebels and preserved the loyalty of the army, he had the opportunity to push ahead with his policy. For a moment he considered activating article 16 of the constitution, which granted the president emergency powers. Instead he asked parliament for a temporary grant of special powers to deal with the aftermath of the insurrection. He also created a Committee for Algerian Affairs, which brought together senior ministers and senior military and civilian officials in Algeria. This committee, which de Gaulle chaired, replaced the Council of Ministers as the main forum for the deliberation of Algerian policy. Its creation increased still further de Gaulle's personal control over the policy.[15]

This bureaucratic initiative apparently reflected a new impatience in de Gaulle's attitude towards the problem. A good indication of what was passing through his mind in the aftermath of Barricades Week is provided by a letter that he wrote to his son in mid-February: 'we had to be done with the impertinent pressure of the European population in Algiers, with the hard core of politicians which was forming in the army, and finally with the myth of "French Algeria" which merely disguises the desire of the "pieds noirs" to maintain their domination over the Muslims . . . The abscess has been burst.'[16] De Gaulle's strident language suggested a fundamentally unsympathetic attitude towards the *pieds noirs* – an attitude which some have traced back to the latters' wartime Vichyism, others to the General's aversion for Mediterranean temperaments or to his incomprehension of the *pieds noirs'* 'tortured double identity – half French, half Algerian'.[17] His stridency also reflected a new perspective on the importance of the whole conflict. On 13 February 1960 France exploded its first atomic device in the Sahara. This was the culmination of an atomic programme that the Fourth Republic had begun and which de Gaulle had accelerated. Coming so soon after the fiasco of Barricades Week, it opened up the prospect of new opportunities in foreign policy and reinforced a determination on de Gaulle's part to liquidate the Algerian problem as soon as possible, even at the expense of major concessions to the FLN and its government-in-exile, the Provisional Government of the Algerian Republic or GPRA.

In the months that followed, de Gaulle pressed ahead with his self-determination policy and explored various openings for negotiation with the GPRA, as well as with FLN leaders from inside Algeria. At first these efforts appeared to be paying off. In June 1960 the GPRA finally accepted his offer of official talks (which they had rejected after the self-determination speech). However, the talks soon broke down, and de Gaulle's efforts to find an alternative Algerian force with which to negotiate proved fruitless. The summer and autumn of 1960 were months of profound malaise, as the hopes that negotiation had provoked turned to disillusionment. Not for the last time during the long process of negotiation with the GPRA, de Gaulle himself seemed depressed by the impasse.[18]

In the end, de Gaulle overcame his depression by breaking the impasse. To do so this time required three steps: new concessions to the GPRA, yet another bureaucratic reform to ensure greater compliance with his policy, and a speeding-up of the political process. On 4 November 1960, he made a fundamental verbal concession to the GPRA by publicly acknowledging the future existence of an Algerian republic. He then created a Ministry of Algerian Affairs headed by a trusted aide, Louis Joxe, who, unlike Debré, was in fundamental accord with his 4 November speech. And, finally, he announced that another referendum would be held in January 1961. This referendum would determine once and for all whether or not the French people supported his self-determination policy.

The purpose of this initiative was to abandon integration. But its effect was to cast serious doubt on the policy of association and to hasten negotiations with the GPRA with a view to total independence. In the referendum of 8 January 1961, seventy-five per cent of the metropolitan population backed de Gaulle's policy, but an equally significant result was the clear majority of Muslim Algerians who followed the GPRA's instructions to abstain. Even before he learned of this result, de Gaulle had decided, on the basis of first-hand observations during his final trip in December 1960, that his original association strategy was dead. Flying back from Algeria, he confided to Louis Terrenoire that the idea of finding a non-FLN third force with whom to strike a deal was now out of the question. Most Muslims were nationalists and supporters of the FLN.[19] From that point on, he resolved to negotiate Algerian independence with the GPRA.

That the crisis was entering its final stage was evident from de Gaulle's public pronouncements. In early 1961 he began talking about the Algerian problem as though it were settled, using terms very similar to those which he later used in his memoirs. He told the French people that Algeria cost France too much and was not worth holding on to. If America or Russia wanted to take over France's place there, they were welcome to it. France had other priorities now: she was in the midst of a dramatic modernization at home, had the opportunity to play a greater role in world affairs, and did not need the distractions of a nineteenth-century problem.[20] In a characteristic show of intellectual bravado, de Gaulle now said that he had seen independence coming for twenty years or more. Since the Brazzaville Conference of January 1944 he had never ceased to believe that 'the populations dependent on us should have the right to self-determination'.[21] This was a more than slightly retouched version of his record. In fact, the very first paragraph of the Brazzaville Conference report had expressly ruled out self-determination as a possibility, and during the RPF years de Gaulle had made fairly explicit statements in favour of preserving the empire.

To the defenders of the French presence in Algeria, these brisk and unsentimental balance sheets of France's interest in Algeria were intolerable. 'A rug salesman,' muttered one integrationist colonel on hearing de Gaulle's comments at an April 1961 press conference.[22] This press conference was the final straw for some officers, including a former Commander-in-Chief, General Challe. After it, Challe decided to throw in his lot with three other retired generals (Salan, Jouhaud, and Zeller) who had been recruited by a group of integrationist colonels to lead a *putsch* against de Gaulle. On 22 April 1961 troops supporting the four rebels seized control in Algiers and arrested the government's representatives. In Paris there was widespread panic, as officials awaited a new Operation Resurrection to evict from power the man whom the original operation had aimed to install. De Gaulle, however, did not lose his composure. If anything, he handled this crisis with more aplomb than the earlier one. He activated article 16 to meet the military emergency and immediately addressed the nation. His broadcast of 23 April was a shorter but equally powerful repeat performance of his address at the end of Barricades Week. He described the coup in superbly contemptuous terms, evoked again the miracle of his own legitimacy and of France's revival since 18 June 1940, and warned that all the nation's achievements since then were jeopardized by this 'odious and stupid adventure'. In the name of France, he ordered all troops to remain loyal and oppose the four generals. The impact of de Gaulle's words, which were transmitted to Algeria via Radio Monte Carlo and picked up by soldiers on their transistor radios, was again critical. From the beginning the *putsch* had been poorly conceived: it had failed to mobilize the support of the *pieds noirs* or to win over the conscript troops, who were the vast majority. After de Gaulle's speech it fell apart.

The *putsch* set back the beginning of negotiations between the French government and the GPRA for a short while, but its ultimate effect was to give new momentum to the talks. To use the same metaphor that de Gaulle had used about Barricades Week, the *putsch* burst the abscess of opposition to his policies within the army. De Gaulle's successful handling of the crisis also carried his popularity with the public to new heights. Both these factors gave him a freer hand to negotiate. At the same time, the very seriousness of the crisis and the desperate resort to terrorism that its ending prompted among the *pieds noirs* made some kind of speedy settlement seem all the more imperative.

When the negotiations with the GPRA began, at Evian, in May 1961, de Gaulle was optimistic that they could be concluded speedily. In fact, it took ten frustrating, often depressing months before the Evian Accords were signed. There were several temporary breakdowns. To keep the GPRA at the table, de Gaulle was forced to agree to a series of major concessions on points that he had long proclaimed non-negotiable: to negotiate solely with the FLN; to drop the demand for a cease-fire before negotiations could get under way; and to give up the Sahara to the embryonic Algerian republic. The French negotiators had very little leverage, because their president had indicated so often and so publicly his determination to reach an agreement as soon as possible. De Gaulle's impatience may well have cost France a concession or two, but from his perspective no concession mattered alongside the imperative of getting out of Algeria. On 8 April 1962, when ninety per cent of metropolitan voters approved the Evian Accords, that overriding objective was finally achieved.

. . .

The Algerian crisis showed Gaullist leadership in all its dimensions. Guiding his entire policy was a sense of perspective, which allowed him to look beyond the immediate impasse and to visualize a future beyond Algeria. This sense of perspective led him to lucid conclusions about the inescapable reality of decolonization and the long-term interests of France, which were better served by accepting decolonization than by resisting it. As he had shown during the German occupation, there was no substitute for an early and accurate reading of the trajectory of events.

Having achieved a necessary detachment from the tumultuous present, de Gaulle used a strategy of calculated flexibility to move towards his objective. Why such flexibility or, to call it what it often was, why such ambiguity or downright duplicity? There were two reasons above all others. The first was that de Gaulle did not know precisely what the future held for Algeria. Certainly he was convinced from the beginning that a solution could only come through Algerian self-determination and the democratically expressed will of the French people. But to ascertain what the Algerian people wanted and what the French people would accept was bound to be a gradual process. Until that became clear, de Gaulle regarded it as essential to keep a number of different options open. A second reason for flexibility was even more fundamental: for all its importance, the Algerian crisis was always subordinated in de Gaulle's mind to the larger issue of French power and prestige. *Grandeur* was impossible without national unity and without an army that was totally loyal to the state. When he allowed his prime minister to make reassuring comments about France's continuing role in Algeria or when he himself encouraged rumours that self-determination was just window-dressing for the UN, he was not merely deceiving people for the sake of his Algerian policy; he was fulfilling what he regarded as one of the state's sacred responsibilities: to keep the fabric of national unity intact.

The tactics that he employed during the crisis were vintage de Gaulle, for better and for worse. As in the Free France years, he combined a tough 'inside game' with very effective public relations. Within his government he maintained strict control over the formulation of policy, a control which tightened as the crisis wore on. Up to the autumn of 1960 the underlying divergences between himself and Debré had not prevented the two of them from working together closely; after de Gaulle's speech in November 1960, the policy became less collaborative and more than ever the exclusive domain of the presidency.

To present his policy to the outside world and defuse opposition to it, he made brilliant use of his personal prestige. Here, his old taste for face-to-face encounters was complemented by his mastery of the new mass medium of television. He profited from a striking convergence between his philosophy of government, which was based on the need to bypass intermediaries such as parties and establish a direct relationship between himself and the people, and a technology which facilitated precisely that kind of personalized and direct communication.[23]

The flaws in his tactics were equally characteristic of his method. For example, his belief that the leader's job was to set a policy and leave his subordinates to implement it – the belief that he had expressed at the War College in the 1920s (see page 4) – got him into deep water in Algeria. Barricades Week revealed the enormous disparity between de Gaulle's policy and the reality of its implementation. Of course, to some extent this disparity had served de Gaulle's purposes by softening the blow of self-determination. Indeed, it had been made possible by the deliberate ambiguity of his pronouncements. Still, there was, at times, an element of complacency in de Gaulle's approach, which proved costly.

Another familiar failing was his distaste for the give-and-take of bargaining. If his remarkable strategic instinct convinced him at an early stage that it would be necessary to negotiate with the FLN, his obvious repugnance at the process caused major problems. Until early 1961, he stuck to an unrealistically hard line about the necessity of concluding a military cease-fire before political talks could begin. After that, he swung to the opposite extreme, preferring to make a series of unilateral concessions rather than 'haggle' with the GPRA. Needless to say, both approaches made life difficult for the officials who were doing the actual negotiating.

. . .

Until the Algerian problem was resolved, everything else remained, in a sense, provisional. That was even true of de Gaulle's other main preoccupation in these years – his ambitious and contentious foreign policy. The purpose of this policy was twofold: to offer new and larger horizons to the French people and to the army, so as to divert attention from Algeria; and to safeguard France's position from outside encroachment until such time as more favourable military and international conditions (an end to the Algerian war and the development of a French atomic arsenal) gave him the opportunity to unveil his long-term strategy.

The new president was fundamentally at odds with the international status quo that he encountered in January 1959. He was suspicious of the bipolar system, which, in his view, increasingly reflected nothing more than the national interests of the two superpowers. He was contemptuous towards the United Nations, critical of the operation of the western alliance, and hostile to supranationalist tendencies in Europe (even though, for pragmatic reasons, he had honoured the Treaty of Rome and taken France into the Common Market). Perhaps the aspect of the postwar settlement to which he could most easily reconcile himself was decolonization, because that at least could be understood within a fundamentally nationalist framework. As de Gaulle told the leadership of the new African state of Mali, 'There is no international reality which is not first of all a national reality.'[24] What was true for the new African states was also true for France. This did not necessarily mean a dramatic change in the substance of French policy: in its last phase the Fourth Republic had asserted French independence through a nuclear policy and a far from submissive attitude towards the US and Britain. De Gaulle's assertiveness represented a change in style rather than a policy revolution.

As in the 1940s, this assertiveness was directed towards allies as much as enemies, on the principle that today's ally might become tomorrow's enemy, and vice versa. De Gaulle at first maintained an attitude of stern disapproval towards the Soviet Union, especially during the protracted Berlin crisis (1958–61). So long as the Cold War continued, he remained convinced of the necessity of a firm response from the West. On the other hand, he regarded Khrushchev's initiatives in Berlin and, later, in Cuba as the final flings of a conflict that was drawing to a close.

More fundamental – because it looked towards a future international order rather than the waning one – was the critique of NATO and American hegemony that he developed on his return to power and that remained one of the hallmarks of his international policy throughout the 1960s. This critique was expressed to British and American leaders as early as July 1958.[25] It was presented formally in a confidential memorandum that he sent to President Eisenhower and Prime Minister Macmillan in September 1958, to 'hoist his colours', as he put it in his memoirs (the same expression that he had used to describe the broadcast of 18 June 1940).[26] Here one sees again one of de Gaulle's favourite techniques: the establishing of an authoritative text (like the Bayeux speech or the self-determination speech) to stake out a position and set his interlocutors on the defensive from the outset.

The message of his September memorandum was straightforward. First, the Atlantic Alliance had to expand its scope to include other parts of the world where western interests might be threatened. It was unacceptable, in his view, that an ally such as the US should feel free to criticize French policy in Algeria.[27] Second, the political and strategic decisions of this global alliance had to be made by an organization that included French representation and did not reserve a monopoly of decision-making to the United States. As he put it in subsequent letters to Eisenhower, since an American nuclear attack would automatically place France in grave danger of a retaliatory Russian attack, France had an absolute right to participate in any decision about such an attack.[28] Third, France's future role in NATO would be contingent on a satisfactory revision of the alliance. So long as the Algerian and Berlin crises were continuing, de Gaulle did not spell out the full implications of this threat, although his decisions, in 1959, to withdraw the French Mediterranean fleet from NATO and to deny the US permission to base atomic weapons in France were clearly designed to reinforce the original message.

While de Gaulle quietly and sometimes not so quietly

chipped away at a NATO defence policy integrated under American leadership, he also sought to assert French autonomy and leadership in Europe. The technique was very similar. Rather than adopting a defensive posture towards the supranational integration that he saw gaining ground, he tried to seize the initiative by developing European cooperation in directions acceptable to France and his nationalist views of French interests.

The European initiatives took two forms. The first was an attempt to establish a privileged relationship with West Germany, to whose existence he had now reconciled himself. In fact, this might better be termed the de Gaulle–Adenauer relationship, since it was a peculiarly personal form of diplomacy. It had been forged at the outset in a very cordial meeting that the two men had at Colombey in September 1958. Thereafter, it was fostered by de Gaulle's staunch support of Adenauer's hard line on Berlin. De Gaulle hoped to gain two benefits from this relationship: to reduce West German dependence on the US; and to form the nucleus of a political confederation, which might ultimately control the activities of existing supranational institutions, particularly the EEC Commission, and redirect the movement for European unity, away from supranationalism.

This idea of a political confederation of the Common Market states – the other dimension of his European initiative – had been in the air since the first meeting with Adenauer in 1958.[29] De Gaulle raised it formally with the Chancellor in July 1960. Adenauer was encouraging and over the course of the summer French and German officials began consultations with officials from the other four nations. In February 1961 a summit meeting of the six Common Market governments agreed to create a commission to make proposals for a political union. This commission, chaired by a Frenchman, Christian Fouchet, began its work in Paris in March 1961 and continued deliberating into 1962. In the end, however, the talks broke down. The French (i.e. the General's) version of an intergovernmental, non-integrationist community was rejected by the Dutch and Belgian governments, because it conflicted with their integrationist ideals and because they objected to de Gaulle's exclusion of Great Britain.

The Fouchet plan's demise did not appear to cause de

Gaulle undue distress, any more than did the Americans' failure to respond to his memorandum.[30] Since these initiatives were primarily holding operations until the Algerian war was over, they had already served their purpose. By the middle of 1962, with the war over and the nuclear programme progressing, de Gaulle could contemplate other, more important initiatives.

Before then, however, he had to pass through a tricky transitional phase at home. 1962 brought another *après-guerre* – a postwar transition which, like the first one in 1945–46, proved full of danger, both personal and political. The threats to his person came from a terrorist organization formed by die-hards of French Algeria and known as the *Organisation Armée Secrète* (OAS). One of the OAS's main objectives was to bring de Gaulle to justice for betraying French Algeria. In September 1961 de Gaulle survived an OAS assassination attempt at Pont-sur-Seine. The following August, in miraculous circumstances, he survived another attempt at Petit-Clamart: fourteen bullets fired from three directions hit the car that he and his wife were riding in.

The political danger was also a real one. In the spring of 1962, with the national emergency now over, the parliamentary opposition came back to life. In April, de Gaulle relieved Debré of the premiership and in his place appointed Georges Pompidou, a man who had never held a seat in parliament. The assembly endorsed the new prime minister by the slimmest of margins. The ranks of government supporters had shrunk from 453 in 1959 to 259 in 1962. There was also increasing criticism of de Gaulle's policies. On 13 June, for example, 296 deputies voted in favour of a supranational political organization for Western Europe, thereby condemning de Gaulle's more state-centred policy. With legislative elections due to be held the following year, de Gaulle knew that he might soon have to face a hostile majority committed to clawing back power from the president.

So, while the OAS plots raised or rather revived concerns about what would happen to the Fifth Republic after its founder's disappearance, the re-emergence of parliamentary opposition revived concerns about a restoration of the *régime des partis*. His narrow escape at Petit-Clamart finally convinced the General that it was time to take action to meet both dangers at once. A week after the attack, he informed his ministers and the country of his intention to modify the constitution. Two weeks later, he announced that a referendum would be held to change the method of electing the President of the Republic, by replacing the electoral college with popular election. The change would take effect at the end of his present term (1965) or before then, if he were to die in office.

Like all his most important decisions, this one had both a long and a short history. In his memoirs he admitted that he had secretly aspired to it for decades, but had not pressed the issue for tactical reasons (because it would have made him vulnerable to the charge of Bonapartism and perhaps also, as Debré argued in his memoirs, because popular election of the president in the circumstances of 1958 would have placed a majority of votes in the hands of the peoples of the French Community).[31] In any case, more than a year before the attack at Petit-Clamart de Gaulle had both publicly and privately floated the idea of a constitutional modification, to increase what he called the 'personal equation' in the president's power.[32] His reasoning was that none of the men who were conceivable successors were of sufficient stature to reign – he talked privately about his 'monarchy' – without the legitimation of popular election. He himself had not needed that legitimation in 1958, because of the special relationship that already existed between General de Gaulle and France. But to prevent the parties from restoring their stranglehold over his successors, it was essential to give future presidents a semblance of authority and power through an electoral mandate.[33]

De Gaulle's interest in this reform picked up noticeably in the spring of 1962, as he began to look for ways of heading off parliamentary moves to reduce his role. If he was going to adopt this strategy, it made sense to do so as soon as possible – before new legislative elections renewed parliament's mandate and while Algeria was still fresh in people's memories. In June he gave a broad hint that he was on the verge of acting. Privately, however, he was still sending conflicting signals to his supporters, some of whom got the impression that he had not decided whether to act.[34] It would seem that the attack at Petit-Clamart did play a role, if only to banish lingering reservations.

The announcement of the referendum provoked a huge storm in the political world. For four years political differences between the president and the parties had been muted because of the war, but now the dikes burst. The controversy immediately focussed not on the substantive issue (although all the major parties apart from the UNR opposed the change) but on the procedure which de Gaulle had proposed. Article 89 of the constitution clearly stated that the constitution could only be revised with the prior agreement of parliament, but basing his decision on article 11 (the clause which gave the president power to hold referenda), de Gaulle decided that the question would be put directly to the people. In the view of an overwhelming majority of the country's constitutional experts and even many loyal Gaullists, this decision was an unconstitutional one. These principled objections were taken up by the General's political opponents, who dusted off the old charge of plebiscitarianism. In protest at de Gaulle's violation of the constitution, the assembly passed a vote of censure on the Pompidou government (5 October). A combative de Gaulle responded by dissolving parliament and calling for new elections (18–25 November). Meanwhile, the referendum campaign was marked by increasingly heated rhetoric on both sides. The parties warned of personal rule and a Salazar-type regime, if de Gaulle were allowed to get away with flouting the constitution and adding to the powers of the president. De Gaulle warned of a return to the bad old days of incoherence and irresponsibility.

An air of unreality hung over the whole campaign. The procedural issues which inflamed the politicians left most voters cold, as they had done seventeen years earlier in the referendum campaign of 1945. Even the constitutional principle itself hardly captured the popular imagination. The real issue with the voters was de Gaulle himself, and the General reinforced that perception by warning that he would resign if the proposed change was rejected or even if it passed by a slim majority. It was clear that the General's opponents were right: this *was* a plebiscite. But it was precisely for that reason that they were likely to lose. The legalism of their arguments ran into a kind of collective common sense, which told voters that it was, after all, *his* constitution and that so soon after the end of the war France still needed de Gaulle. This sense of his irreplaceability was reinforced at the last moment by the dramatic and threatening events of the Cuban Missile Crisis, which began just six days before the French voters went to the polls.

In the end, de Gaulle's margin of victory in the referendum of 28 October 1962 was less impressive than he had hoped for: only sixty-two per cent of those who voted approved the change. Any disappointment that he felt did not last long, however. The relatively small majority (relative to those of earlier referenda) convinced him of the need to enter the fray in the general election campaign. On 7 November, he appealed to the voters to support Gaullist candidates. This appeal proved a resounding success. In the elections later that month, the Gaullist parties (UNR and UDT) won 229 seats, close to an absolute majority. With the support of various independents, they gave the General a solid working majority.

De Gaulle had clearly created this confrontation, but it would be misleading to suggest that his courting of it represented a fundamental change in direction, either in ideology or method. Ideologically, it was a return to his roots – to his obsession with the innate hostility of what he called 'les féodalités' (political parties, trade unions, special interest groups) towards the state. The methods that he employed in September and October 1962 – the referendum combined with a personal appeal to popular confidence and official manipulation of the mass media – were essentially those he had employed throughout the early years of the Fifth Republic. In each of the referendum campaigns since his return (September 1958, January 1961, April 1962), the government had manipulated the outcome as much as it decently could in a democratic system.[35] The official position had dominated the broadcasts of the RTF (*Radiodiffusion et Télévision Française*). Last-minute concessions had been made to disaffected groups to win their support. The official envelopes sent to voters with their ballot papers had contained sheets giving de Gaulle's reasons for a 'yes' vote (but never any reasons for a 'no' vote). And de Gaulle had, on each occasion, made strong personal appeals for a large 'yes' vote, implicitly and sometimes explicitly indicating that he would resign if the vote went against him. So, if his tactics in October 1962 were perhaps more blatant than in the past, they were certainly far from unprecedented.

What was different in October 1962 – and accounted for the drop in the 'yes' vote and the bitterness of the debate – was that this time the referendum was not taking place in wartime. The earlier referenda had been plebiscites, but, in a sense, non-partisan plebiscites in which the vast majority of metropolitan voters had identified de Gaulle's position with the national interest. This was clearly a partisan plebiscite. At stake was not the resolution of a desperate national emergency, but a choice between two fundamentally different concepts of democracy, the outcome of which was bound to affect the trajectory of French politics for years to come.

. . .

NOTES AND REFERENCES

1. Hoffmann S 1974 Last Strains and Last Will: de Gaulle's 'Memoirs of Hope', *Decline or Renewal? France since the 1930s*. Viking, New York, pp. 259–62.
2. De Gaulle C 1970 *Mémoires d'espoir* (2 vols). Plon, Paris, vol. 1 pp. 49–50.
3. Lacouture J 1985 *De Gaulle* (3 vols). Le Seuil, Paris, vol. 2 p. 439.
4. Rudelle O 1988 *Mai 58: De Gaulle et la République*. Plon, Paris, p. 113.
5. Ageron C-R 1980 *'L'Algérie algérienne' de Napoléon III à de Gaulle*. Sindbad, Paris, p. 245.
6. Terrenoire L 1964 *De Gaulle et l'Algérie*. Fayard, Paris, p. 41.
7. Lacouture J 1985 vol. 2 pp. 570–1.
8. LNC vol. 8 pp. 183–4; Massu J 1972 *Le Torrent et la digue*. Plon, Paris, p. 196.
9. Droz B, Lever E 1982 *Histoire de la guerre d'Algérie*. Le Seuil, Paris, p. 220; Lacouture J 1986 *De Gaulle* (3 vols). Le Seuil, Paris, vol. 3 pp. 64–5; Tricot B 1972 *Les Sentiers de la paix*. Plon, Paris, pp. 103–6.
10. Tricot B 1972 p. 114.
11. Boissieu A de 1982 *Pour servir le général 1946–1970*. Plon, Paris, p. 114; Droz B, Lever E 1982 p. 231; Massu J 1972 p. 286.

12. Flohic F 1979 *Souvenirs d'Outre-Gaulle*. Plon, Paris, p. 34.
13. Lacouture J 1986 vol. 3 p. 86.
14. Letter of 21/1/60, LNC vol. 8 p. 318.
15. Tricot B 1972 pp. 142–3.
16. LNC vol. 8 pp. 330–1.
17. Jackson J 1990 *Charles de Gaulle*. Cardinal, p. 65.
18. Debré M 1988 *Mémoires* (3 vols). Albin Michel, Paris, vol. 3 p. 260.
19. Terrenoire L 1964 pp. 215–17; Ageron C-R 1980 p. 250.
20. Press conference of 11/4/61, DM vol. 3 pp. 287–94; speech of 12/7/61, DM vol. 3 pp. 327–32.
21. DM vol. 3 p. 289.
22. Lacouture J 1986 vol. 3 p. 158.
23. Guichard J-P 1985 *De Gaulle et les mass media*. France-Empire, Paris, p. 109.
24. Speech of 13/12/59, DM vol. 3 p. 153.
25. Ledwidge B 1984 *De Gaulle et les Américains*. Flammarion, Paris, pp. 26–9.
26. The memo is reprinted in LNC vol. 8 pp. 83–4. Word of its existence leaked out at the time, but the full text was not published until the 1970s.
27. Alphand H 1977 *L'Etonnement d'être*. Fayard, Paris, p. 304.
28. Letters of 25/5/59, 6/10/59, LNC vol. 8 pp. 225–8, 263.
29. Couve de Murville M 1971 *Une politique étrangère, 1958–1969*. Plon, Paris, pp. 37, 40.
30 Burin des Roziers E 1986 *Retour aux sources: 1962, l'année décisive*. Plon, Paris, p. 59.
31. De Gaulle C 1971 *Mémoires d'espoir* (2 vols). Plon, Paris, vol. 2 pp. 17–20; Debré M 1988 vol. 2 pp. 405–6.
32. Press conference of 11/4/61, DM vol. 3 pp. 301–2; letter of 4/6/61, LNC vol. 9 pp. 93–4.
33. Flohic F 1979 p. 58.
34. Guichard O 1980 *Mon général*. Grasset, Paris, pp. 385–6.
35. Williams P 1970 *French Politicians and Elections 1951–1969*. Cambridge, pp. 97–8, 115–18, 130–9.

Chapter 7

1963–67: SOVEREIGN

In the Gaullist world-view, the best of times were always potentially the worst of times. Success in any great enterprise brought with it the danger of complacency, the danger that the French would surrender to their demons of fragmentation and mediocrity. No sooner had de Gaulle ended the Algerian nightmare and registered his political triumphs in late 1962 than he became morbidly apprehensive of such a national relapse. Its shadow was to hang over the remainder of his presidency. When the first round of presidential elections in 1965 gave him a less than overwhelming endorsement, he concluded morosely that the French were no longer afraid of anything and were slipping back into 'dispersion' and 'facilité'.[1]

As usual, de Gaulle's language was loaded: 'dispersion' really meant pluralism; 'facilité' meant the French people's understandable impatience to begin enjoying the rewards of twenty years' hard work. But beneath his rhetoric lay an indisputable truth about the era of the mid-1960s. For the only time in his career (with the arguable exception of the months between May 1945 and January 1946) de Gaulle was not confronted by an all-consuming national or international crisis. The earlier phases of his career had been dominated by the Second World War, the Cold War and the threat of a Third World War, and the Algerian War. The final phase was to be dominated by the upheavals of 1968. The years in the mid-1960s, with their relative tranquillity and affluence as well as political stability, were an anomaly. If they afforded unique opportunities, especially in the international realm, they also posed the ultimate challenge for him: to elevate the banality of peace and prosperity into something epic.

He met this challenge by manufacturing a sense of drama through his theatrical style of rule and through his ambitious policies. Whatever their nominal aim, all the policies which will be discussed in this chapter were intended to keep France on the high road towards *grandeur*. Not surprisingly, such policies had costs. Of course, Gaullists claimed that the General's policies had always had costs. But the question which began to be asked more often after 1962 than before was: were the costs worth it? Was the *éclat* of his foreign policy worth its economic price? Did political stability justify the pretensions and excesses of his republican monarchy? Did the quest for a modernized infrastructure and low inflation rates justify meagre improvements in living standards for many of the French people? Without a national crisis to provide an overarching justification for his brand of leadership, de Gaulle's actions increasingly became subject to more normal political criteria. No doubt that was why some Gaullists saw 1962 as the high point of the General's career and the years that followed – in some respects the apogee of his republican monarchy – as a protracted decline.[2]

. . .

Throughout the 1960s, politicians kept up a rather futile polemic as to whether the General cared about anything except foreign affairs. Critics charged that he was too busy thinking about France to concern himself with the problems of the French people. The General and his supporters retorted that 'for France to be strong, the French must be prosperous'.[3] De Gaulle's own words, however, gave the game away: his objective was for France to be strong, and the prosperity of the French was a means to that end. It was not the case that he neglected domestic issues – least of all in the period 1963–65 – but rather that he saw them within the larger framework of France's relations with the world.

The General's chief preoccupation between 1963 and 1967 was to transform these relations and to transform the bipolar international system that regulated them. To be understood in its own terms, his policy should be seen not as the implementation of a 'vision' of some future world order radically different from anything existing at the time, but as a series of practical initiatives to accelerate and to exploit an already occurring transformation. De Gaulle believed that the Cold War, which had frozen not just the superpowers but the rest of the world in a paralyzing confrontation between two blocs, was coming to an end and that, within each bloc, the hegemony of the respective superpower was dissolving. In Western Europe, old nations had rebuilt themselves, economically and militarily, and were increasingly combining their resources. In the 'totalitarian world', as de Gaulle called it, a rift had opened up between Beijing and Moscow, while the nations of Eastern Europe were showing signs of restlessness. In the Third World new nations were flexing their muscles for the first time. It was within this evolutionary framework that de Gaulle situated his policies. The term 'Gaullist design', which has often been applied, is perhaps misleading. De Gaulle was more interested in exploiting the process of change (in the interests of France and of his regime) than in forcing it to a fixed end-point. Indeed he was probably uncertain himself as to what the end-point would be, except that it was bound to be a less rigid and less bipolar system than the old one; and he assumed that a more flexible multipolar system would not only be more advantageous to France but would be safer and more equitable for all states.

De Gaulle had long made clear his dissatisfaction with the Cold War status quo. Before 1962 he had attempted to modify it through at least five distinct initiatives: by sponsoring a political confederation of Western European states; by proposing a restructuring of NATO; by fostering a special relationship with the Federal Republic of Germany; by decolonizing and establishing new connections with Third World nations; and by pushing ahead with the development of France's nuclear weapons programme. The final two initiatives were to continue in the years ahead, but the other three had reached or would shortly reach the end of their trajectory. The European confederation had been vetoed by France's European partners. The restructuring of NATO had been repeatedly vetoed by two American administrations. The Paris–Bonn axis, it is true, was about to be formalized, with the signing of the Franco-German treaty in January 1963, but it quickly became clear that the Federal Republic was not willing to make this axis the basis of its foreign policy. In place of these old initiatives, de Gaulle now switched to a more assertive and unilateral strategy, in which he did more of the vetoing.

His initial steps were taken to foil what he interpreted as attempts by the superpowers or their proxies to bolster the bipolar order. In a dramatic press conference in January 1963 he vetoed two important Anglo-American initiatives. First, he announced his opposition to Britain's application to join the Common Market. The crux of his reasoning was that British connections with the Commonwealth, with European states outside the EEC, and with the United States would transform a cohesive European community into a larger and looser Atlantic community under American control. Second, he turned down a proposal from the Kennedy administration to create a Multilateral Nuclear Force (MLF), in which British and French nuclear forces would have been integrated with some American forces under NATO command. At a meeting in the Bahamas the previous month President Kennedy had persuaded the British prime minister, Harold Macmillan, to agree to the MLF in return for American Polaris missiles. De Gaulle rejected the same deal, in part because it was not, in fact, the same deal. France had not been a party to the negotiations, had not enjoyed the same privileged access to US nuclear technology, and possessed neither the submarines to launch Polaris nor the warheads to arm them. More important, it was unthinkable, on grounds of principle, for France to give up control over her own nuclear arsenal, whatever compensations might be offered in return.

The MLF proposal, as de Gaulle saw it, was the latest in a series of ploys to dissuade France from developing her own nuclear capability. It was also, like the British application to join the EEC, viewed as an attempt to reassert Anglo-American, i.e. American, hegemony on the continent. At this stage, de Gaulle still held out hopes that he could rally Western Europe, especially West Germany, against this hegemony. In rejecting the MLF he pointedly challenged the reliability of the American nuclear umbrella for Europe, now that the US was vulnerable to Soviet retaliation.

His implication was that the French 'strike force' ('force de frappe') would provide a more credible deterrent and could, therefore, protect Western Europe more effectively than the infinitely larger American arsenal. This strategy appeared to receive a boost a week after his conference, when Chancellor Adenauer came to Paris to sign the Franco-German treaty. In fact, however, the signing of this treaty proved to be the last hurrah of de Gaulle's West European strategy. When Bonn soon realigned itself with Washington, de Gaulle was compelled to look for other ways of resisting American hegemony in the West. There were two options: he could either take unilateral measures to challenge US hegemony or he could seek alternative partners with a common interest in breaking down hegemonic control. Over the next five years he tried both options.

The unilateral option took the form of a long-running campaign against both the economic–financial power of the US and its political–military dominance within NATO. The campaign against American economic and financial power began in earnest in 1963. Early in the year, de Gaulle approved a policy aimed at restricting American takeovers of French companies.[4] In a press conference in July he raised the 'problem of the dollar' for the first time, while behind the scenes he listened sympathetically to proposals (emanating from Jacques Rueff, among others) for reform of the international monetary system.[5] These proposals were first aired publicly by the French government at the annual meeting of the IMF in September 1964. They acquired a wider notoriety five months later, when de Gaulle decided to champion them in a press conference (4 February 1965). On that occasion, he criticized the existing monetary system, the so-called gold exchange standard, on the grounds that it was skewed in favour of the United States. Because the dollar had a privileged status as a reserve currency, theoretically interchangeable with gold, the United States was free to run up huge balance of payments deficits, print money to cover these deficits, and then export their inflation through foreign investment, in the process buying up foreign companies. To remedy this bias, de Gaulle called for a return to a system based on gold, which would discipline US monetary policy and place

119

all nations on a more equal footing. His campaign against the dollar, however, had to be fought largely on a rhetorical plane. Though he had gained some leverage by systematically converting France's dollar holdings into gold ever since 1959, it proved impossible to disengage from monetary integration without the cooperation of France's EEC partners, which was not forthcoming.

The scope for genuinely unilateral action was much greater in the political–military realm, especially once the huge army that had been fighting in Algeria had been re-patriated and re-equipped. By early 1965, de Gaulle was contemplating his ultimate gesture of 'anti-hegemonism': total withdrawal of French forces from NATO. In January 1965 he told his ambassador in Washington that at some point before the Atlantic treaty came up for renewal in 1969, he would end integration of French forces and order all foreign forces to leave French soil.[6] It would not be the end of France's participation in the alliance – although privately de Gaulle toyed with that step[7] – but the end, so far as France was concerned, of participation in the structures and institutions of NATO. Later in the year he conveyed the same message to the visiting American Under-Secretary of State, George Ball.[8]

Why he chose not to act until the following March is unclear. A commonly held view is that he delayed with-drawal for political reasons, until after the presidential elec-tions of December 1965.[9] Equally it might be argued that since withdrawal from NATO was the last card he could play in his campaign against American influence, short of defecting from the West altogether, there were good reasons not to play it until it seemed likely to be effective or became absolutely necessary. Both conditions had been met, in de Gaulle's mind, by early 1966. Withdrawal was necessary because the American war in Vietnam appeared to the General to be on the verge of widening into a larger conflict. This scenario brought out all de Gaulle's fears of being dragged by military and political integration into a war that France did not wish to fight. Withdrawal was likely to be effective – or, at any rate, more likely than in the past – because the totalitarian world had begun to break up and there were new possibilities for France to explore outside the West.

Here the unilateral option intersected with the other strategy that de Gaulle had been pursuing, in a number of places, over the course of the previous three years. In the Third World, he had devoted considerable energy to developing special relationships based on French aid, cultural links, and a mutual commitment to the principle of national independence. The high point of this campaign came in the autumn of 1964, when he made a highly publicized tour of ten Latin American countries, in which he repeatedly denounced the imperialist tendencies of the superpowers. An even more important link, in terms of international power politics, had been forged in January 1964, when he established diplomatic relations with the People's Republic of China. This step was a significant move in its own right, since de Gaulle saw China as one of the emerging giants of the new multipolar system. It was also a display of independence from Washington that was meant to be noticed elsewhere, particularly in Moscow.

Within a few months, for the first time in more than a decade, observers began to detect a thaw in Franco-Soviet relations. At first, it was hardly dramatic: a couple of cordial official visits and commercial agreements. It began to accelerate in February 1965, when de Gaulle stated publicly that a definitive resolution of the German problem could only be achieved through an understanding of all Europeans, west and east.[10] This pronouncement, and the changed policy it conveyed, set the context for a serious effort at *détente* with the eastern bloc (the Soviet satellites as well as the USSR itself). What de Gaulle offered was not merely peaceful coexistence between the two halves of Europe, but a dissolution of both blocs and, in their place, the 're-establishment' of a European *ensemble*, stretching from the Atlantic to the Urals. De Gaulle's hope was that France's withdrawal from NATO would act as a catalyst and speed up the process of change within both blocs.

That did not occur, however. In spite of de Gaulle's relatively successful trip to the Soviet Union in June 1966, the Franco-Soviet *détente*, like the alliance with West Germany and the diplomatic relations with China, produced few tangible results. Having played his last major card without success, de Gaulle's strategy seemed to lose coherence. In the second half of 1966 and throughout 1967, rhetorical attacks on American policy in Vietnam, which he had been making since 1963, intensified. In September 1966 he travelled to Cambodia to denounce American intervention in the region. In December he described the war in Vietnam as 'unjust' and 'detestable'.[11] Increasingly he seemed fixated on the danger that it would escalate into a world war. When a new Arab–Israeli crisis broke out in May 1967, the General linked it closely to the war in Asia and predicted to Harold Wilson that the world might well be at war by September.[12]

There was no world war by September, but what did occur was the first major decline in the domestic popularity of his foreign policy. One commentator described it as the moment when de Gaulle's spell was broken.[13] Two events were responsible: the Six Day War in the Middle East (June 1967) and the General's trip to Canada (July 1967). In the Middle East crisis de Gaulle adopted a specious and unpopular neutrality. In advance of the fighting he warned both sides not to take military action, even though Egypt's prior closing of the Straits of Tiran was widely regarded as itself an act of aggression. He also called unsuccessfully for concerted action by the US, USSR, France, and Great Britain, and announced an arms embargo to all belligerents. The latter hurt Israel far more than the Arab states because France had long been an important arms supplier to Israel. De Gaulle's policy was clearly motivated by a concern to preserve France's newly improved relations with the Arab world, but it was perceived as hostile to Israel and unfriendly to the West as a whole. The accusation of hostility to Israel took on new meaning in November 1967, when de Gaulle made comments about the characteristics of the Jewish people that were interpreted as anti-Semitic.

Even more damaging to his popularity was the controversial visit to Canada. On 24 July, at the end of a triumphal progress through the province of Quebec, de Gaulle addressed the people of Montreal from the balcony of the city hall. It was his seventeenth speech in two days. He was tired and undoubtedly moved by the warmth of his welcome. Even under such circumstances, he was not a person to blurt out words that he did not mean. So when he concluded his speech with the slogan of the Quebec separatist movement – 'Vive le Québec libre!' – he probably did so deliberately. Historians who have reconstructed the context of his trip have generally concluded that, far from being a momentary aberration, the Montreal speech was the culmination of a policy that can be traced back to the early 1960s. For several years, the General had been convinced that French Canada was moving inexorably towards an assertion of its French identity and towards separate statehood. He had long believed that France's duty was to do everything possible to favour this evolution. The extraordinary fervour of his welcome apparently convinced him that this was the moment to act.[14] In doing so, he naturally infuriated the federal government in Ottawa, which protested that his words were an intrusion into Canada's internal affairs. In the wake of the protest, de Gaulle announced that he was cutting short his visit and returned immediately to Paris. There his trip was widely viewed, even by members of his government, as an embarrassment. The French press was extremely critical, and opinion polls showed that only eighteen per cent of voters approved of what he had done, while forty-five per cent disapproved.[15]

. . .

Evaluating this set of foreign policies is no easy task. While appreciating the sophistication and fluidity of de Gaulle's conceptions, one cannot overlook the extreme reactions they provoked at the time or the extensive and mostly critical academic literature that has grown up around them since then. Perhaps the place to begin is with the critics. More than any other policy at any other stage in his career, de Gaulle's foreign policy in the mid-1960s has been comprehensively criticized – in concept, operation, and outcome.

The basic conceptual flaw, according to 'Anglo-Saxon' politicians, lay in its anachronistic assumptions. It was based on a nostalgia for the epoch of 'la grande nation', impossible to recreate under the conditions of the twentieth century. De Gaulle was often depicted as a Don Quixote tilting at windmills or King Canute trying to turn back the waves, while the reality was that France was a middle-sized power with no prospect of returning to its Napoleonic glories. The multipolar system he aimed to create was viewed as another anachronism. In 1958 Harold Macmillan called him Rip Van Winkle, because he talked about the 'Concert of Europe' and 'seemed not to have quite realised what had happened to the world since the end of the Second War'.[16] There was some truth in the Don Quixote jibe, but de Gaulle was no Rip Van Winkle: his multipolar system was not a return to the past but an updated, global version of the nineteenth-century European system.

Rather than accusing him of anachronism, academic critics tended to concentrate their fire on internal contradictions or flawed assumptions in his policy. The major contradiction that they detected was between his vision of a European *ensemble* able to challenge the two existing superpowers and his narrowly nationalist priorities. It has been suggested that his revisionist objective of French greatness was impossible to reconcile with his revolutionary objective of a new multipolar system.[17] Critics also assailed the policy's assumptions from a number of different directions. Atlanticists attacked what they saw as a false parallelism in de Gaulle's treatment of the two superpowers. Raymond Aron, for example, argued that the General's policy 'accustomed the French to taking on the wrong enemy'.[18] Stanley Hoffmann argued that de Gaulle underestimated the resilience of Soviet ideology in Russia and Eastern Europe, and as a result 'out of wishful thinking and premature anticipation, imagined in Russia a far greater move away from totalitarianism at home, a greater willingness to let a "hundred flowers" bloom in Eastern Europe . . . than existed'.[19] Alfred Grosser challenged de Gaulle's assumption that Great Britain was the American 'Trojan Horse' in Europe – a role which in many respects belonged more to West Germany.[20]

Then there were various criticisms of the policy's implementation. Many argued that the General's unilateral style antagonized unnecessarily. The classic case of this was his veto of British entry into the EEC in 1963. By the time that he announced his decision, many Europeans were reaching the conclusion that Britain's terms for joining the Market were unacceptable. What infuriated not just the British and Americans, but also France's five EEC partners was the manner in which, without consultation, de Gaulle announced a *fait accompli* 'as though France were somehow the custodian of the Community's purity'.[21]

Another sore point was de Gaulle's fondness for theatricality and rhetoric, which sometimes came at the expense of substance. Rather than railing against American policy in Vietnam in 1966–67, might he not have attempted to mediate a solution to the conflict?[22] Rather than warning Arabs and Israelis not to attack one another, might he not have used his influence in Arab capitals to resolve the problem in the Straits of Tiran? Some critics suggested that he was more concerned to be vindicated by posterity than to achieve actual results. Others even reached the conclusion that there was no Gaullist design at all. 'It was all performance, played for its own sake against a dazzling background of reflecting mirrors . . . [with] little real content.'[23]

Finally, many critics pointed to the policy's actual failures and costs. De Gaulle failed to break down the barriers between West and East in Europe. As the events of the 'Prague Spring' in 1968 were to demonstrate, he failed to loosen Moscow's grip over its satellites. He failed to convert France's relations with the Third World into a decisive asset. He failed to end the dollar's supremacy or America's predominant influence in Western Europe. Worse still, his policy often proved counterproductive for Europe as a whole and for France. Only a unified Western Europe was truly capable of challenging American hegemony, but the consequence of de Gaulle's stubborn nationalism was to make such unification impossible. It was narrow self-interest, according to his critics, which led the General to veto Britain's entry into the Common Market: in Macmillan's words, 'he wants to be the cock on a small dunghill instead of having two cocks on a larger one'.[24] Even more damaging to the larger cause of Europe were de Gaulle's continuing efforts to restrict supranational integration. These efforts came to a head in 1965, when for seven months France boycotted the EEC Commission and Council of Ministers and thereby precipitated one of the gravest crises in the Community's history. Though the crisis was eventually resolved (by the so-called Luxembourg Compromise of January 1966) and though de Gaulle largely succeeded, in the short term at least, in blocking supranationalism, his policy was widely deplored as a blow to European unification. Some saw a tragic irony in this, since they suspected that de Gaulle was the only person 'with the necessary authority to head a Europe that desperately wanted his leadership'.[25]

The costs for France were also considerable. The obsession with independence and resisting American hegemony had economic costs. To give one example, the restrictive policy towards American investment between 1963 and 1966 drained capital away from France into the economies of her European partners/competitors.[26] There were also social and ultimately political costs. More important than the actual resources that the policy of *grandeur* diverted from domestic problems was the damaging impression it created – an impression that the regime was more concerned about foreign policy than domestic problems.[27] For all the popularity of the policy itself, de Gaulle was never able to convince voters that international issues were more pressing than domestic ones. His attempt to do so fostered a current of resentment that came to the surface in 1968.

Most of these criticisms were made in the 1960s and 1970s. More recent events in the Soviet Union, Eastern Europe, and Central Europe have cast de Gaulle's policy in a different and more favourable light, however. They have largely vindicated his belief in the tenacity of national identities and the superficiality of ideological systems. They may yet vindicate his vision of Europe from the Atlantic to the Urals. But the fact that part of de Gaulle's prediction seems, more than two decades later, to have been borne out by events is only a partial defence of his policies – unless one subscribes to the view of his critics that he was more interested in being vindicated by posterity than in achieving results in his lifetime. Certainly the role of Cassandra had its temptations for him, especially towards the end of his life. But his policy as a whole was much more than mere posturing. In the 1960s his foreign policy had two concrete and not unrealistic aims: to solidify a national consensus around the themes of *grandeur* and independence; and to advance France's interests within a bipolar world in transition.

In the first aim, de Gaulle was quite successful. His foreign policy attracted support from across the political spectrum. Indeed his stance on some issues, like the Vietnam War and *détente* with the East, attracted leftists more than conservatives. The result was a broad consensus around the ideals of a strong France, an independent Europe, and a transformed Third World. It is hard to tell exactly how heavily domestic political motives weighed with de Gaulle. By virtue of his unique personal prestige, he himself was relatively insulated from the pressure of public opinion. There is every reason to believe that he would have pursued his policy even if it had been unpopular (as it temporarily became in 1967). On the other hand, he was concerned not just for his own popularity but for the legitimacy of his regime, in general, and of the presidency, in particular.[28] He clearly hoped and expected that the consensus around his foreign policy would rub off on the presidency, reinforcing perceptions of its national and non-partisan function. These expectations were realized.

In his second aim he was far less successful. The large transformations that de Gaulle sought did not occur, and the concrete achievements proved of limited significance. The root of many of the failures lay in de Gaulle's impatience. He returned to power in 1958 haunted by the thought that he was ten years too late.[29] There was an increasing sense of 'now or never' in his actions. Initiatives such as the Montreal speech and even the withdrawal from NATO were motivated in part by a feeling that he could not trust his successors to do the necessary. This impatience led to an overestimation of the potential for change and to premature and ill-fated attempts to force its pace. France was simply too weak a power – in military, economic, or political terms – to pull this off.

We may presume that, if the events of 1989 had taken place in 1965, not only would de Gaulle's prophetic powers have been universally recognized, but as a result France's influence in the world would have been dramatically enlarged. But the fact was that the world did not change as de Gaulle had predicted. Without external evidence of a transformation, other states had little or no reason to follow de Gaulle's lead. The uninspired prophet cut a rather lonely and ultimately inconsequential figure.

. . .

In the domestic field, it is more difficult to talk about the General's – as opposed to his government's – policy. The reason is not that he ignored domestic issues. On the contrary, he concerned himself with them more in these years than before 1962. In his public appearances, he boasted tirelessly about the miracles of economic and social progress that had already been achieved and proselytized about the necessity of further modernization. Inside the government, he kept a close eye on the development of policy and frequently intervened to prod ministers in desired directions. However, these interventions were less systematic than those in foreign policy. Moreover, many of them were made with the aim of preserving achievements from an earlier period (particularly, the stable currency and low inflation). On domestic issues he had a less clearly defined reform agenda of his own. Where he did have strong personal views, he proved less willing or less able to implement them over the opposition of others.

Essentially, his message to the French people in the mid-1960s was: more of the same. Economic success in the long term required further sacrifices in the short term. In line with this philosophy, the Fourth Plan (1962–66) and the Fifth Plan (1966–70) gave highest priority to investing in the economy's infrastructure, modernizing industrial equipment, and consolidating French businesses into larger and more competitive units. For the consumer this meant deferred gratification.

Similarly, the consumer (and taxpayer) bore the brunt of de Gaulle's absolute insistence on preserving the value of the franc. When inflation began to rise in 1963, the General intervened personally to instruct his prime minister and minister of finance to prepare a 'stabilization plan'. The plan raised taxes, restricted credit, and introduced price controls. It was supposed to last six months but remained in effect for more than two years. Though it succeeded in slowing inflation, it also slowed growth and became increasingly unpopular. De Gaulle, however, defended it not just in economic terms but on the grounds that inflation would imperil the franc and throw France on the mercy of foreigners. 'Certainly, it is a burden. 1,500 years of history have taught us that to be France is not without its difficulties, its risks, or its costs.'[30]

There was an obvious incongruity between this heroic, patriotic rhetoric and the reality perceived by most French men and women, which was a reality of partisan, tight-fisted policies.[31] This incongruity was exposed in the spring of 1963 during a famous miners' strike. De Gaulle took a hard line towards the strike. He encouraged the government to requisition the workers, and signed the order himself. This order was simply ignored by the strikers, however, and in the end the government was forced to compromise, while de Gaulle's own popularity fell to the lowest point of his entire presidency. In the short term, the damage was not too serious. The General's popularity soon rebounded, largely because voters tended not to associate unpopular aspects of his government's domestic policy with him and because his foreign initiatives were generally well received. But in the longer perspective the events of 1963 had demonstrated a profound dialogue of the deaf between the strikers, who had chanted 'Charlot, des sous!' ('Pennies, Charlie!'), and the General, who had responded by evoking 1,500 years of French history.

The political implications of this dialogue of the deaf did not become fully apparent until the presidential elections of 1965. In the long run-up to these elections de Gaulle maintained a calculated uncertainty about his future. The valedictory tone of certain press conferences as well as his ostentatious promotion of Pompidou to the status of heir apparent encouraged speculation about a retirement. Whether or not he seriously contemplated stepping down is, in fact, unclear. We do know that it was not until the late summer of 1965 that he gave private indications of his intention to stand for a second term,[32] and not until 4 November that he made his decision public. His reasons for standing again may be surmised. First, important elements of his international agenda would have been left unfulfilled, had he not run. Second, he could not have been certain that any successor he designated – even Pompidou – would have been elected in December. Indeed, it is perfectly plausible that one of his political enemies – such as his former minister Pinay or the leftist François Mitterrand – would have succeeded him. Third, he could not have failed to be reassured by the rising trend in his own popularity, which suggested (to him at least) that, in spite of grumbling about the stabilization plan, the people were still ready for the 'high road'.

Having announced his candidacy, de Gaulle withdrew to a position of proverbial reserve. He did not campaign and at first declined to make use of the television time allotted to each of the candidates. This proved an unfortunate strategy. Out of a crowded field of candidates, two serious challengers emerged: Mitterrand, the candidate of the left, and Jean Lecanuet, a Christian democrat who used Europeanist themes to win conservative and centrist support. Mitterrand and Lecanuet portrayed the General's refusal to campaign as contempt for the democratic process. They denounced the regime as a system based on personal power, and in Kennedyesque terms suggested that a man born in the nineteenth century was out of touch with contemporary concerns. Television helped both main challengers project themselves as serious and qualified candidates for the presidency, while accentuating the contrast between their youthfulness and the tired, out-of-touch grandfather in the Elysée. As opinion polls and other reports showed de Gaulle's support slipping – from a high of sixty-nine per cent before the campaign to forty-three per cent on the eve of the elections – his advisers and ministers urged him to enter the fray. At the last moment he did so. But it was too late. On 5 December he received 44.6 per cent of the vote and was forced into a runoff election against Mitterrand, who had come second with 31.7 per cent.

He later admitted that that evening 'a wave of sadness' swept over him and he seriously considered withdrawing.[33] The result was disappointing because it so patently contradicted his claim to be a truly national leader. It left him with two alternatives. Either he could cling to that myth of the national leader, in which case the logical step was to resign and hold himself in reserve for another national crisis. Or he could jettison the myth and run in the second ballot as the leader of the majority, which was what he had in effect been since October 1962. It did not take him very long to decide in favour of the second course. He was seventy-five years old. It was too late to start the cycle of withdrawal and reserve again. On 8 December he told his ministers that he had blundered by treating the election as a referendum and would not make the same mistake again. This time, he agreed to be a candidate in the fullest sense of the term. The high point of his campaign came in three lengthy and unscripted television interviews with a sympathetic journalist.[34] De Gaulle's animated presentation and common touch in these interviews were disarming. His willingness to talk to the French people on their level was received as a touching gesture rather than a condescending one. The interviews helped to bolster his position and on 19 December he won a comfortable though hardly crushing victory (fifty-five to forty-five per cent).

The cost of becoming a candidate, all observers agreed, was that thereafter de Gaulle was more widely viewed as a partisan figure. That perception only added to the urgency with which he threw himself into new international initiatives. In foreign affairs, 1966 and 1967 were perhaps the most hectic years of his presidency. On the domestic front, the General turned over more power to Pompidou than he had done before 1965, although he did not abandon domestic politics entirely. In the campaign for the legislative elections in March 1967, he spoke on behalf of the Gaullist party and orchestrated the government's presentation of its record.[35] And after the elections, which returned the slimmest of Gaullist majorities, he tried to broaden his constituency by reviving the reformist theme of worker participation. For the most part, however, he found more to preoccupy him outside France (where he feared the imminent outbreak of a global conflict) than inside. In December 1967, he wrote to his son: 'Nothing much new in Paris. Politically, socially, and economically, the year is ending calmly, so far as our country is concerned.'[36]

. . .

At a press conference shortly before the presidential elections in 1965, de Gaulle had defended himself and his regime against the accusation of 'personal power'. He began on a note of defiance: 'If what is meant by that is that the President of the Republic has personally taken the decisions which it was incumbent upon him to take, that is entirely correct.' Then came a characteristic note of banter: 'who ever believed that General de Gaulle . . . should content himself with opening flower shows?' Finally, he let the 'facts' speak for themselves: 302 Council of Ministers meetings, 420 Interministerial Council meetings, 505 audiences with the prime minister, 2,000 meetings with individual ministers, 1,500 meetings with senior civil servants or experts, 30 televised addresses to the nation, 12 press conferences, visits to 94 departments, 2,500 communes, and so on.[37]

This list proved that de Gaulle was not a reclusive autocrat, but it hardly dispelled – indeed its tone corroborated – the perception of a republican monarchy. Others gave advice, but he decided. In private, de Gaulle was quite explicit that this system of government amounted to a form of monarchy. On at least one occasion, he went so far as to express the hope that his own son would succeed him as monarch.[38] A thorough analysis of the regime's operation lies beyond the scope of this work, but since the years between the referendum of 1962 and the great crisis of 1968 marked the high point of this monarchy, it is appropriate to say more about de Gaulle's own role in it.

To understand de Gaulle's monarchy, one must begin with the man himself, since he believed so firmly that policy should reflect an individual will rather than an ideology or a process of political bargaining. It was, of course, the case that his decisions, like anyone else's, reflected ideological presuppositions and bureaucratic and political constraints. But it has to be said that he tried more consistently and more self-consciously than most political leaders to insulate himself from external pressures and to personalize decision-making.

The first and most critical stage in his exercise of power was the formulation of a 'will'.[39] This process began with a phase of intense and extended reflection, in which he could deploy his formidable gifts of intellectual curiosity and comprehension. His reflection was fed by information from a wide variety of sources – from the presidential staff at the Elysée, from his ministers, from officials and experts, from the abundant official documentation that passed across his desk, and from the media (he read all the major French newspapers as well as the *Daily Telegraph*, the *Frankfurter Allgemeine Zeitung*, and the *New York Herald Tribune*, and his normal weekday routine always ended in time for the eight o'clock television news).[40] Given his professed contempt for journalists, the importance of this last source was surprising, but all the more revealing about his determination to keep informed and up to date. His information-gathering was active rather than passive. When he discussed an issue with somebody, his characteristic method was to pepper his interlocutor with questions or observations, trying out ideas or arguments before they were definitively formed. Similarly, he read pen in hand, constantly writing notes to his staff or commenting on other people's notes.[41] When he had gathered enough information to feel in command of an issue, he required peace and quiet to order his thoughts, assimilate the information within the framework of his part-instinctual, part-rational world-view, and reach a decision. His routines were organized so as to facilitate this intellectual process: weekends were reserved for Colombey, where he could take long walks and mull over problems; workday schedules at the Elysée were strictly adhered to; he insisted on absolute punctuality and an atmosphere of unruffled calm.

The formulation of a decision was quite distinct from its implementation, which often did not take place until months or even years later. The first process set a general objective which was valid whether or not it could be attained under existing circumstances. The second was essentially a matter of timing. The key was to act at the moment when conditions were most conducive to the course upon which de Gaulle had decided. This separation between decision-making and actual implementation might appear rigid, but in fact de Gaulle was flexible enough to recognize that conditions could change between the moment of decision and the moment of implementation and that sometimes these changes were fundamental enough to require a modification of the original decision. Whatever its pitfalls, he viewed this procedure as infinitely preferable to the procedure of most other politicians, who tended to make snap decisions without advance preparation, often on the basis of an accommodation between competing interests. Bargaining and impromptu decision-making, both of which he abhorred, were, in his mind, inextricably linked.

Within the government de Gaulle's military training shaped his exercise of power. He believed in the chain of command: he communicated with civil servants through their ministers and (with occasional exceptions) with ministers through the prime minister;[42] and he did not regard it as his function to supervise the actual process of implementing decisions. On the other hand, he had the last word whenever he cared to have it, not just on foreign or defence policy but on any aspect of policy. If a decision that he regarded as properly belonging to himself was taken at a lower level (even by the prime minister), he invariably administered a sharp rebuke. The essence of presidential power was its unpredictability: the General could intervene at any moment and on any issue.

The discretionary power that de Gaulle gave his prime ministers varied over the course of his presidency. Debré had assumed wide powers over domestic policy-making during the Algerian War. Between 1962 and 1965, de Gaulle reclaimed a more active role in domestic policy, partly because he now had the time to do so and partly because Pompidou, who had never held elective office, had a more presidentialist conception of the constitution than Debré. After the presidential elections in 1965, the situation partially reverted to that of 1959–62. That said, one must be careful to distinguish power from authority. More or less power could be delegated from the Elysée to the Matignon (the prime minister's residence), but authority always rested at the Elysée. As de Gaulle put it in a controversial passage at one press conference: 'The President is obviously the only person to hold and to delegate the authority of the State.' (31 January 1964).[43] This was not the arbiter-president that Debré and the other drafters of the constitution had anticipated, but rather a ruling president who was not necessarily constrained by the letter of the constitution (as he showed in his frequent recourse to referenda and in his willingness to replace prime ministers at his, rather than the assembly's, pleasure).[44]

One of the clearest indications of de Gaulle's supremacy over the collective executive was the role of the Council of Ministers. Under de Gaulle, the Council's main function was to ratify decisions that had already been approved, if not made, by him. He personally oversaw and, if necessary, modified the agenda for meetings. During the meetings ministers were not expected to raise objections to decisions affecting other ministries, much less to challenge the chair. If they did so – as Antoine Pinay did in a famous 'scene' in November 1959 – they were rebuffed.[45] On only three or four occasions in his entire presidency did de Gaulle permit frank exchanges and an open debate in the Council of Ministers.[46] On some vital decisions – for example, the withdrawal from NATO – ministers were only informed collectively after the fact.[47]

Consigning the Council of Ministers to this dignified but pro forma role created the need for an alternative forum in which to discuss and coordinate policy. The constitution had provided for such an alternative – the Cabinet Council in which ministers met without the president under the chairmanship of the prime minister. Debré had held frequent Cabinet Councils in 1959 and 1960, but after 1961 the institution lapsed.[48] De Gaulle apparently did not care to give ministers an opportunity to make important decisions without his supervision. Instead, he increasingly resorted to the device of the *ad hoc* Interministerial Council, in which the prime minister and relevant ministers, along with senior military or civilian officials, were invited to the Elysée to consider a specific problem or area of policy. During Debré's premiership, these councils had been limited to defence issues, Algeria, and African affairs. But after mid-1962 they proliferated and considered a wide range of domestic and international issues.[49]

De Gaulle used the Interministerial Councils in order to inform himself more fully on important issues or to give momentum to policies that he favoured. It was not coincidental that Interministerial Councils played a particularly prominent role in the formulation of economic and financial policy. This was an area where decision-making demanded particular expertise (which, although he was a diligent learner, de Gaulle did not possess) and where the danger of his surrendering control to experts was correspondingly great. The Interministerial Council was an indispensable tool for keeping track of his own government and ensuring that it followed the line that he delivered from above.[50]

In general, de Gaulle was acutely aware of the danger of being boxed in by his own institutions and losing the capacity to act *as an individual* and to exert his personal will. He guarded against this danger in a number of ways besides the bureaucratic device of the Interministerial Council. One was by cultivating the non-partisan persona of General de Gaulle and distancing himself whenever possible from the political party upon which his government depended. For instance, when he stood for re-election in

1965, his campaign was run by the 'Association Nationale Pour le Soutien de l'Action du Général de Gaulle', not by the UNR. In the run-off campaign, he chose longtime followers like André Malraux, rather than Gaullist politicians like Pompidou, to present his case.

His public pronouncements – drafted with infinite care, painstakingly memorized, and then delivered with a minimum of improvisation – were another, even more effective, method of asserting personal leadership. Whatever their text, the subtext was always this: this is *my* will. Needless to say, in a complex modern government that was usually a simplification, but one which served two powerful purposes: to sustain popular confidence in his leadership and to give the state itself a clear sense of direction.

This assertion of individual leadership took place in a number of settings. In addition to making highly publicized provincial or foreign tours, he appeared frequently on French television (ninety-one times in all between 1958 and 1969). But the most important setting was the semi-annual televised press conference, a ritual which was aptly described as the high mass of the regime and in which the role of the press was, to say the least, negligible. The importance that the General attributed to these events may be deduced from the enormous pains he took to prepare for them. Typically he would break his normal routine for several days in order to write and commit to memory his lengthy 'answers' to pre-determined questions. Since the conferences lasted an hour and a half or longer and some of his individual answers took twenty-five minutes to deliver, this was a prodigious effort. The conferences always took place in the same room (the Salle des Fêtes in the Elysée) and followed a very formal procedure. They were attended not just by journalists but by senior civil servants, foreign diplomats, and – seated to the right of the General – the prime minister and the other members of the government. De Gaulle turned these occasions into major political events in their own right. They were preceded by weeks of speculation (some of it inspired by the Elysée) and followed by weeks of commentary and exegesis, all of which had the effect of focussing journalistic and public attention on the presidency.

· · ·

The achievements of this republican monarchy by 1967 were indisputable. De Gaulle's foreign policy had restored a level of national self-respect and consensus that had been absent since the First World War. Under his leadership, the French economy had maintained the impressive economic growth begun under the Fourth Republic, and combined it with far greater financial and monetary stability. The comparative performance of the French economy may be judged more or less favourably, depending on the criteria and the time-frame used, but over the decade of the 1960s as a whole it grew at an average annual rate that matched or surpassed that of most of France's main trading partners.[51] It would only be reasonable to give at least some of the credit for this successful adaptation to de Gaulle's incessant proselytizing about the necessity of modernization.

There could be no doubt that he deserved the credit for the republic's political consolidation. As promised, his regime had delivered a degree of governmental stability that France had not enjoyed for many years. A sharp contrast between this record and the immobility and instability of the Fourth Republic undoubtedly existed in the minds of many citizens and gave the regime a broad base of support.[52] Perhaps more important, since memories of the bad old days were bound to fade sooner or later, was the progress he had made towards transforming the strong presidency from a crisis expedient into a permanent and widely accepted feature of French political life. In general terms, the monarchical presidency – with its combination of assertiveness abroad, pageantry and preachifying at home, and lofty detachment from daily politics (for which the prime minister took responsibility) – proved a successful formula. More specifically, the presidential elections of 1965, while disappointing from a personal standpoint, had vindicated the constitutional revision of 1962; de Gaulle's opponents had campaigned in a presidential style quite different from that of the Fourth Republic.

Yet, in retrospect, there were also warning signs for de Gaulle. The autocratic style of a president who regarded state-controlled radio and television as a transmission service for the government, who felt free to interpret his constitution as he saw fit and regularly to circumvent parliament or his own ministers teetered perpetually on the verge of excess. This became an issue in 1967, as a result of his unpopular initiative in Canada. In August of that year, his former finance minister, Giscard d'Estaing, warned of the dangers of 'the solitary exercise of power'. The potential victims of this autocracy were not only liberal democratic values, but also effective government. As Philip Williams and Martin Harrison noted, 'the superimposition of republican monarchy on the structure of cabinet government meant that the chain of decision-making was often uncertain. It was often hard for the minister or civil servant . . . to know when normal procedures might be disrupted by a sudden intervention from the Elysée.'[53] The problems that this could cause were to be demonstrated all too vividly in 1968.

The loss of reformist energy on the domestic front was another potential problem (as de Gaulle seemed to acknowledge in returning to the old theme of participation in 1966–67). The regime's tendency to conservatism was all the more serious because it coincided with huge socio-economic upheavals associated with modernization and the coming to maturity of the postwar baby boom. Between 1960 and 1965, for example, the French population aged fifteen to twenty years increased by forty per cent. Transformations of that magnitude necessitated transformations in numerous social and educational institutions. Although de Gaulle recognized as much, he and his regime made little progress in that direction, and it is surely too simplistic to lay the entire blame for this failure at Pompidou's door (as the General's admirers are inclined to do).

Finally, for all the majesty of his presidential rule, de Gaulle himself had undergone at least a partial 'desanctification' in the years after 1962. This did not mean a dramatic drop in popularity: indeed, his approval rating was higher in 1966 and early 1967 than it had been at any point since the Algerian crisis. Instead, desanctification meant a growing tendency to treat him as a politician 'like the others'. The social crisis of 1963 had shown that de Gaulle was not immune to traditional sources of political dissatisfaction. The elections of December 1965 and March 1967 had confirmed what had been clear in the elections of 1962: that his political base was, in fact, partisan rather than truly national. Ever since 1947 some Gaullists had recognized that the General's willingness to prolong his role beyond periods of acute crisis – the only periods in which he could function as a consensual leader – risked compromising his mystique. In 1968–69 their fears were finally borne out.

. . .

NOTES AND REFERENCES

1. LNC vol. 10 p. 221.
2. Noël L 1976 *De Gaulle et les débuts de la Ve République.* Plon, Paris, p. 284.
3. Television interview of 13/12/65, DM vol. 4 p. 414.
4. Kuisel R 1990 De Gaulle's Dilemma: The American Challenge and Europe. *French Politics and Society*, **8** (4): 13–24.
5. Prate A 1978 *Les Batailles économiques du général de Gaulle.* Plon, Paris, pp. 207–8.
6. Alphand H 1977 *L'Etonnement d'être.* Fayard, Paris, pp. 443–4.
7. Note of 23/2/65, LNC vol. 10 p. 134.
8. Ball G 1982 *The Past Has Another Pattern: Memoirs.* Norton, New York, pp. 332–3.
9. Chantebout B 1979 Le Retrait de l'O.T.A.N., in *'L'Entourage' et de Gaulle.* Plon, Paris, pp. 235–6.
10. DM vol. 4 pp. 337–42.
11. DM vol. 5 p. 130.
12. Wilson H 1971 *The Labour Government 1964–1970. A Personal Record.* Weidenfeld and Nicolson, pp. 402–6.
13. Charlot J 1971 *Les Français et de Gaulle.* Plon, Paris, p. 86.
14. Lescop R 1981 *Le Pari québécois du général de Gaulle.* Boréal Express, Montreal.
15. Charlot J 1971 p. 281.
16. Horne A 1989 *Harold Macmillan, II, 1957–1986.* Penguin edn, p. 113.
17. Kolodziej E 1974 *French International Policy under De Gaulle and Pompidou: the Politics of Grandeur.* Cornell UP, Ithaca.
18. Aron R 1983 *Mémoires.* Julliard, Paris, p. 449.
19. Hoffmann S 1974 De Gaulle's Foreign Policy: The Stage and the Play, the Power and the Glory, *Decline or Renewal? France since the 1930s.* Viking, New York, p. 325.
20. Grosser A 1967 *French Foreign Policy Under De Gaulle* trans L A Pattison. Little, Brown, Boston, p. 115.
21. Marjolin R 1989 *Architect of European Unity. Memoirs, 1911–1986* trans W Hall. Weidenfeld and Nicolson, p. 338.

22. Mendès-France P 1989 *Oeuvres complètes* (6 vols). Gallimard, Paris, vol. 5 pp. 223–4.
23. Newhouse J 1970 *De Gaulle and the Anglo-Saxons.* Viking, New York, p. 48.
24. Horne A 1989 p. 446.
25. Ball G 1982 p. 97.
26. Kuisel R 1990 p. 22.
27. Hoffmann S 1974 p. 323.
28. Cerny P 1980 *The Politics of Grandeur: Ideological Aspects of de Gaulle's Foreign Policy.* Cambridge, pp. 245–69.
29. Lacouture J 1986 *De Gaulle* (3 vols). Le Seuil, Paris, vol. 3 p. 557.
30. Speech of 28/9/63, DM vol. 4 p. 136.
31. Larkin M 1988 *France Since the Popular Front.* Oxford, p. 304.
32. Lacouture J 1986 vol. 3 pp. 622–5.
33 Interview of 7/6/68, DM vol. 5 p. 296.
34. DM vol. 4 pp. 412–40.
35. Letter of 12/2/67, LNC vol. 11 pp. 74–5.
36. LNC vol. 11 p. 167.
37. DM vol. 4 pp. 390–1.
38. Letter of 12/4/64, LNC vol. 10 p. 52.
39. Tricot B 1977 Le Processus de prise des décisions, in *De Gaulle et le service de l'Etat.* Plon, Paris, pp. 119–58.
40. Blanc P-L 1990 *De Gaulle au soir de sa vie.* Fayard, Paris, p. 155.
41. 1979 'L'Entourage' et de Gaulle p. 163; 1977 *De Gaulle et le service de l'Etat*, pp. 86–7.
42. 1979 'L'Entourage' et de Gaulle p. 162.
43 DM vol. 4 p. 167.
44. Williams P, Harrison M 1973 *Politics and Society in de Gaulle's Republic.* Doubleday, Garden City, NY, pp. 203–42.
45. Andrews W 1981 The Collective Political Executive under the Gaullists, in Andrews and Hoffmann (eds.) *The Fifth Republic at Twenty.* SUNY Press, Albany, pp. 38–9.
46. Lacouture J 1986 vol. 3 pp. 23–4.
47. 1979 'L'Entourage' et de Gaulle p. 236.
48. Andrews W 1981 pp. 26–7.
49. Tricot B 1979 Les Conseils restreints à l'Elysée du temps du général de Gaulle, in *'L'Entourage' et de Gaulle*, pp. 164–72; Burin des Roziers E 1986 *Retour aux sources: 1962, l'année décisive.* Plon, Paris, pp. 41–2.
50. Prate A 1978 p. 21.
51. Prate A 1978 p. 163.
52. Williams and Harrison 1973 p. 428.
53. Williams and Harrison 1973 p. 431.

Chapter 8

1968–69: THE RECKONING

On 28 April 1968, in one of those comments that seem obligatory for a sovereign on the eve of revolution, the General confided to an aide that he was growing bored: 'there is no longer anything difficult or heroic to do.'[1] The storms surrounding the Six Day War and French Canada had subsided. After a poor year in 1967 the economy was showing signs of renewed strength, and de Gaulle's approval rating in polls was back above sixty per cent. Like other countries France was experiencing a wave of student unrest, but there was no reason to suspect that this unrest would threaten the regime's stability. For de Gaulle the main challenge left in 1968 was to make something of his long-cherished plan for worker participation in management. After disappearing from view during his first term, participation had re-emerged to become the major domestic objective of his second term. But by April 1968 de Gaulle had been able to make little headway on this front, confronted as he was by the scepticism of most Gaullists – not least Prime Minister Pompidou – the staunch opposition of employers, and tepid interest on the part of organized labour.

Five days later, when student demonstrations spread from the University of Paris campus at Nanterre to the Sorbonne and the streets of the capital, de Gaulle at first saw no reason to alter his assessment of the banality of the times. From the Elysée the demonstrations appeared to be simple outbreaks of student rowdiness ('le chahut') which the General ascribed to a few agitators and general pre-exam jitters.

141

Events soon dispelled such complacency. On the night of 6–7 May 1968 students and police clashed in bitter street-fighting, which left four hundred demonstrators and two hundred policemen injured. The scene was repeated four nights later, when students erected barricades and the paramilitary CRS was ordered in to clear the streets. In spite of opposition from the communist-led trade unions (CGT), there were also signs of growing collaboration between students and workers. On 13 May a huge demonstration of students and non-students marched through Paris chanting 'Dix ans, c'est assez!' and 'Au revoir, mon général!'

On 14 May wildcat strikes began to break out throughout the country. The same day de Gaulle left for a state visit to Romania. At the last moment he considered postponing the trip, but was persuaded by Pompidou and Foreign Minister Couve de Murville that a visit to the most independent of the eastern bloc states was too important to defer and that the circumstances at home were not serious enough to warrant postponement. The decision was a mistake. By the time de Gaulle returned on 18 May, the country was at a total standstill. His subsequent attempt to regain control of the situation by announcing a referendum only made matters worse. In the last week of May, the regime was crumbling before the nation's astonished eyes and de Gaulle himself seemed old, out of touch, and almost irrelevant.

In the end, on 29–30 May, de Gaulle found a way of reasserting his authority. Once he had done so, the 'revolution' fizzled out and a pronounced reaction set in. Gaullism not only survived, but emerged, at the end of June, stronger than before the crisis. General elections returned a huge Gaullist majority to the new assembly. Assimilating the May events into Gaullist mythology, the General told the nation that it had had a bout of collective vertigo on the ascent towards *grandeur*, had almost plunged back into the abyss, but at the last moment had pulled itself together.[2] For de Gaulle himself, however, the events of May 1968 were a disaster from which there proved to be no recovery. He spent the final ten months of his presidency trying to undo the damage that had been done not just to his regime but, above all, to his own image and authority.

This final stage in his career was not the pathetic decline that Pétain and Churchill had suffered and that de Gaulle had always feared for himself. For all his hesitant and maladroit handling of the May events, there is no compelling evidence that his powers of intellect or judgement were gravely impaired. What overtook de Gaulle was in a sense worse than a decline, which at least casts no retrospective shadow on earlier achievements. De Gaulle's final year in office was a period of reckoning in which the failings of his over-centralized, socially conservative regime were exposed and he himself was forced to face the reality that his mythology had lost much of its resonance and his historic role had run its course. There is every reason to believe Madame de Gaulle when she remarked after her husband's death in 1970: 'He suffered so much the last two years.'[3]

. . .

When the troubles began, de Gaulle's first instinct was to take a hard line with the students. Throughout the first week of the crisis, during which Pompidou was out of the country, de Gaulle urged the Acting Prime Minister Louis Joxe and the other ministers not to give in to student demands, not to reopen the Sorbonne, and to crack down on the one per cent of radicals who, as he put it, were terrorizing the vast majority of sheep.[4]

This hard line was modified in practice by other Gaullist instincts which asserted themselves almost at once. One was the reformist instinct that told him to identify an underlying cause of the crisis and to see it as an opportunity to advance his own agenda. As early as 8 May, de Gaulle told his son-in-law, Alain de Boissieu, that the demonstrations reflected a cultural malaise in industrial society which he had been warning against since 1941 and which could only be alleviated by giving individuals more power over their own lives. He predicted to Boissieu that he would be able to use the crisis in the universities to break down the last pockets of resistance to his participation schemes.[5] That indeed was to become his strategy after his return from Romania.

The other instinct at work in early May was the old desire to distance himself from events that he could not control. While he instructed his ministers to be firm with the students, he declined to take personal responsibility for managing the crisis and refused to make any public pronouncement about it. As he told Boissieu, it was not the head of state's job to keep order in the streets. When Pompidou returned to Paris on 11 May, this pattern continued. De Gaulle turned over complete control of the situation to his prime minister, agreeing at once to Pompidou's plan for reopening the Sorbonne. And then, after announcing that he would address the nation ten days later, he flew off to Romania.

Why did de Gaulle remain aloof from what was patently, by that stage, a very serious crisis? He later answered this question by saying that the crisis had still been, in his view, 'insaisissable' (difficult to grasp). A great deal of significance has been read into his use of this adjective: if de Gaulle could not yet grasp what was happening in his country, that showed just how out of touch he was. In his version of the May events (a decidedly self-serving version), Pompidou depicts a tired and discouraged General who could not understand how 'in a prosperous France . . . with everything going well, there could be this kind of disenchantment and brutal desire for change'.[6]

This image of an elderly president perplexed by the demands of a generation half a century younger than himself has become one of the stereotypes of the May events. In fact, although de Gaulle was as perplexed by certain aspects of this generational revolt as anybody else his age, his problem was not really one of comprehension *per se*. As we have seen, by early May he had formed his own view of the underlying social causes of the crisis – perhaps not the right view, but at any rate one that made sense to him and that conformed to his long-standing intuitions about the flaws in modern industrial capitalism. What de Gaulle meant by 'insaisissable' was not that he could not understand intellectually what was happening, but that he could not take charge of the situation politically in such a way as to draw out the constructive forces he believed to be latent in it. He saw himself as a reformer, but it was not clear how he could advance the cause of reform while it was identified with rioters throwing Molotov cocktails and ridiculing all authority, not least his own. Alternatively, how could he restore order when the 'enemy' were not *pied noir* die-hards or Muslim nationalists but the sons and daughters of the French bourgeoisie and millions of ordinary French citizens, middle class as well as working class?

It was during the trip to Romania, as the news being relayed to him from France got steadily worse, that he settled on a course of action.[7] On 16 May he told Couve de Murville that he had decided to go before the French people with an ambitious plan of social reform, to institute participation in the university, in the workplace, and in local government. This proposed renovation of French society would have to be approved in advance, by referendum. Nothing could have been more characteristically Gaullist than the conceit of being more revolutionary than the revolutionaries (just what he had claimed to be in 1944) and the tactic of using a referendum to reassert his personal authority not just over street insurgents but over his own conservative-minded party. In the circumstances, however, there was something uncharacteristically a priori about the strategy. There is evidence that he had been contemplating a referendum on participation ever since the legislative elections of March 1967; if so, he had simply decided to do what he had been intending to do all along.[8] Rather than resolving the crisis and then using the energies released by it to further his own objectives (as he had done successfully on several occasions during the Algerian War), he had apparently convinced himself that furthering his own objectives would resolve the crisis. He was putting the cart before the horse.

And yet de Gaulle knew as well as anyone that reform could only follow the restoration of order. When he returned from Romania, he was infuriated by the chaos that he found and immediately ordered his government to clear the Odéon theatre which had been occupied by students on 15 May and to purge the O.R.T.F. (state-run broadcasting service) of government critics.[9] He summed up his reaction in a comment released to the press: 'La réforme, oui; la chienlit, non!' Nobody quite knew what to make of 'chienlit' (literally 'shit in the bed', figuratively a shambles or carnival), but it was clearly derogatory.

Having sounded this tough note, however, de Gaulle was persuaded by ministers and advisers that a policy of forcible evacuation from the Odéon or the Sorbonne would almost

certainly lead to huge casualties. So the 'chienlit' continued. To go ahead with reform under such conditions contradicted his own instincts and ran the risk of appearing
weak. De Gaulle chose to take the risk for reasons about
which we can only speculate – perhaps he was desperate to
reclaim the political momentum, perhaps he overestimated
his own prestige or the popular appeal of the reforms that
he intended to propose. In any case, he appeared on radio
and television on 24 May, as announced, to explain his
views about the necessity of a 'mutation' in French society
and to declare that a referendum would be held in June to
give the government authority to renovate the university
and the workplace. The speech failed disastrously. The students immediately ridiculed the 'old uncle's' tame attempt
to be progressive. The General's supporters, who had expected him to deliver a stern law and order message, were
appalled by his talk about participation and reform. Nobody was satisfied by the ritualistic recourse to a referendum. '[I]t seemed,' wrote Raymond Aron, 'as if we were
listening to the phantom of a spectre or the spectre of a
phantom.'[10]

There are various explanations for the fiasco of the
24 May speech – a fiasco which he immediately sensed and
which was reflected, in succeeding days, in a precipitous
decline in his popularity.[11] Some generous souls have
argued that the speech might have worked if he had
delivered it immediately on his return to France. They
suggest that the delay was fatal, since it allowed the situation
to drift further out of control and created impossibly high
expectations about what de Gaulle could do.[12] All agree
that he appeared old and tired and that the text was not
forceful enough to reassure the bourgeoisie or to inti-
midate the demonstrators. But, having said all that, the
root of the failure lay deeper. The speech fell flat because
its message of participation via referendum, by which de
Gaulle proposed to remedy the ills of French society and
recreate a national consensus, fell flat. The bourgeoisie
and political conservatives were hostile to it; the General's
opponents were profoundly uninterested in it.

In retrospect, 24 May did prove an important turning-
point in the crisis, but not because of anything that de
Gaulle said and partly because of what he did not say. That

evening, for the first time, rioting broke out on the Right Bank as well as the Left. The Stock Exchange was set on fire – a potent symbol to a bourgeoisie already disconcerted by de Gaulle's speech. There is some evidence that from this point Parisian opinion, which had been relatively indulgent towards the demonstrations (more indulgent than provincial opinion), swung against them.[13]

After his failed initiative, de Gaulle was not in a position to benefit from this reflex. Instead, Pompidou, who had appeared the most dynamic and competent member of the executive throughout the crisis, found himself in an even stronger position. On 25 May Pompidou began negotiations with the representatives of the trade unions and employers, with the aim of buying his way out of the crisis by giving workers immediate wage increases. While Pompidou negotiated, de Gaulle seemed a marginal figure. At the Council of Ministers meeting on 27 May, ministers were struck by how distracted and depressed he looked.[14]

Reconstructing de Gaulle's mood in these extraordinary days, when the regime that he had built seemed to be caving in around him, is essentially a matter of guesswork. Plenty of people saw him and recorded their impressions. Most were struck by his depression. But impressions such as these are almost impossible to evaluate. Ever since his London days, de Gaulle had had a habit of affecting an apocalyptic air in order to disconcert or test his supporters. In this instance it would seem safe to assume that he indeed passed through a phase of discouragement. Nothing could be much worse for a person of his colossal pride than to be ridiculed in the streets of his capital and to be eclipsed by his own prime minister. We can also be certain that at some point between 24 May and 30 May he emerged from this phase of discouragement and decided to fight out the crisis. Some witnesses, notably Pompidou and General Massu, have suggested that there was a sudden transformation in his attitude on 29 May, in circumstances that will be recounted below. Others have argued that the transformation came a day or two earlier. A more plausible explanation is that there was no sudden change, and that he contemplated withdrawing throughout the week, even as a new strategy and a new resolve germinated in his mind.

De Gaulle's willingness to recognize the error of his previous strategy was an essential first step in the new direction (as it had been after the first round of the presidential elections in 1965). Once he had taken it, events seemed to come to his aid. Pompidou's negotiations with the CGT produced an agreement (27 May), which was promptly disowned by the strikers. In an attempt to regain control over the movement, the communist leaders announced a massive demonstration in Paris for 29 May. Meanwhile, François Mitterrand, de Gaulle's opponent in 1965, publicly declared that 'if power became vacant' he would be a candidate for the presidency and, if elected, would appoint Pierre Mendès-France prime minister. For the first time in the crisis the political opposition was emerging into the open to lay claim to the post-Gaullist succession. In the process they presented de Gaulle and his government with a far more inviting target to strike at than the nebulous movement of students and strikers.

Georges Pompidou recognized the opportunity at once. When the communists announced their demonstration, the prime minister immediately ordered military precautions against a potential coup – which privately he did not expect to happen[15] – and gave the go-ahead for a Gaullist counter-demonstration on 30 May. On 28 May he informed de Gaulle of these measures and predicted that if all went well the government would soon be in a position to end the crisis. According to Pompidou, the General's response implied that he was not so sanguine.[16] Indeed, there is every reason to believe that de Gaulle *was* less sanguine than his prime minister. Pompidou had been overly optimistic throughout the crisis, and de Gaulle had just had to comfort his wife, who had been verbally accosted in the streets of Paris that afternoon. But it seems unlikely that a political tactician of de Gaulle's skill failed to recognize the opportunity that the opposition leaders' actions presented. Circumstantial evidence suggests that, on the evening of 28 May, he was already pondering how best to take advantage of that opportunity.

This brings us to the events of 29 May 1968, one of the most controversial and frankly bizarre days in de Gaulle's career. The chronology of what happened on that day is now fairly well established, but its significance is still the

subject of much debate. In the morning, a few hours
before the communist march began, de Gaulle postponed
the Council of Ministers' meeting that was due to be held
that afternoon. He told Pompidou that he was tired and
needed a day's peace and quiet at Colombey to gather his
thoughts. What Pompidou did not know was that the
General had instructed his son-in-law to go to Colombey
and from there to telephone General Massu, the former
paratroop commander in Algiers who was now Commander
of French Forces in Germany, to arrange a rendezvous with
de Gaulle later that afternoon (perhaps in Strasbourg). De
Gaulle had also instructed another officer to take his son
Philippe and Philippe's family to General Massu's headquarters at Baden-Baden. Having made these preparations,
de Gaulle and his wife left the Elysée and were driven to a
helicopter which took off towards the east. The helicopter
did not fly to Colombey, however. Instead it landed at
Saint-Dizier, fifty kilometres north of Colombey. Apparently,
de Gaulle had originally hoped that at that point Boissieu
would be able to tell him where to fly for the meeting with
Massu. But because of a telephone strike Boissieu had not
been able to get through to Massu, and de Gaulle decided
to go directly to Baden-Baden, ordering the pilot to fly at
rooftop level so as to avoid radar. Back in Paris, meanwhile,
the prime minister was informed that de Gaulle had not
arrived at Colombey and that his helicopter had
disappeared. For almost two hours, which he stretched to
four or five in his memoirs, Pompidou did not know where
his president was or what he was doing.

In fact, de Gaulle had landed at Massu's headquarters
and was having a light lunch and a tête-à-tête with his
general. De Gaulle told Massu that he feared the situation
in France was lost and that the communists were about to
seize power. At some length Massu urged de Gaulle not to
quit but to return to Paris and restore order. After an hour
or so, de Gaulle stood up and told Massu that he would
follow his advice. At 4.30 in the afternoon he and Madame
de Gaulle climbed back into the helicopter to fly to
Colombey. They had been at Baden just ninety minutes
and left their son Philippe and his family behind. After
spending the night at Colombey, cheered no doubt by the
news that the communist demonstration had passed off

peacefully, de Gaulle returned to Paris. When he took the chair in the Council of Ministers on 30 May, all agreed that he looked a changed man.

The question was: who or what had changed him? There was no doubt in Massu's mind that the man who had landed at his headquarters on 29 May had been going through a genuine crisis and that he had come to Baden to seek refuge with an old comrade.[17] Madame Massu told her husband that the de Gaulles had brought so much luggage that they had clearly been contemplating an extended stay. Adding this evidence to that of his own eyes and ears, Massu concluded that he had singlehandedly reinvigorated de Gaulle and persuaded him to return. That was the version of events that he communicated shortly afterwards to the minister of defence and to Pompidou.[18] The image of a discouraged de Gaulle on the verge of resignation was naturally consoling to the prime minister, who had been humiliated and infuriated by de Gaulle's deliberate deception.

But from the outset there were those who questioned Massu's account – not necessarily its factual veracity, but the interpretation that he had placed on events – and who believed that de Gaulle had merely been feigning resignation. There is first-hand testimony to support this hypothesis of a ruse. Both Boissieu and the aide who flew in the helicopter with the de Gaulles have suggested that de Gaulle's aim was to take himself and his family out of the reach of the communist demonstrators in Paris, plunge the public into uncertainty so as to regain their attention and loyalty, and reassert his authority over Pompidou and the government.[19] According to this view, which has been favoured by historians, the trip to Baden-Baden was a piece of calculated melodrama designed to reclaim centre-stage. Another hypothesis, much discussed at the time, was that de Gaulle had gone to sound out Massu's loyalty, in case he should have to employ French troops against a revolutionary uprising in France. Although Massu himself was adamant that de Gaulle did not raise any such topic,[20] it is clear that the army's attitude was one of his major concerns at the time.

All in all, it is wise to be sceptical about any black and white interpretation of de Gaulle's actions on 29 May. Even those witnesses who question Massu's image of a totally dejected de Gaulle acknowledge that the General was contemplating a range of options, including resignation.[21] More important, de Gaulle himself later acknowledged publicly that he had been 'tempted to stand down'.[22] Conversely, Massu's account of the General being completely transformed by an hour's pep talk seems inherently implausible, unless de Gaulle was far more profoundly depressed or disoriented than we now realize. More plausible is the scenario of a man who had begun to see his way out of the crisis but still needed to reassure himself that he was on the right track. Massu's words probably did have an impact – at any rate de Gaulle later gave Massu generous credit for his intervention – but even more decisive, one suspects, was the exhilaration of the day itself – the cloak-and-dagger preparations, the knowledge that in Paris rumours would be flying and people would be panicking, the theatricality of the unexpected arrival and the simulated conversion.

Back in Paris on 30 May, de Gaulle brushed aside Pompidou's offer of resignation and read him the text of a speech that he had drafted that morning and planned to deliver the same afternoon. The tone and content of this speech, which was broadcast only on radio, was utterly different from that of 24 May, and in most respects far more to Pompidou's liking. In forthright language, de Gaulle evoked his own legitimacy and then made a series of announcements: he told the nation that he had decided to remain in office, to retain Pompidou, to defer the referendum, to dissolve the National Assembly, and to hold a general election (the decision to call an election, according to most accounts, had been forced on de Gaulle by Pompidou). To justify these measures, he raised the spectre of a communist conspiracy: 'France is indeed threatened with dictatorship. They want to force her to resign herself to a power which would be established in the midst of national despair, a power which would then obviously and essentially belong to the victorious party, that is to say totalitarian communism.' This was the Gaullism of 1947 rather than 1940, but it worked. French citizens who had experienced the initially enchanting but increasingly terrifying sensation of a complete absence of authority were ready for a strong lead.[23] Exactly on cue, the 'stern schoolmaster . . . [had]

whistled an end to fun and games'.[24] That evening, half a million relieved demonstrators marched down the Champs-Elysées, chanting 'De Gaulle n'est pas seul'.

The radio address marked the final turning-point in the crisis. All the political parties, including the PCF, switched their energies to the elections. Within a couple of days the strike movement and the student demonstrations began to subside. The mood of reaction which had set in at the end of May gained strength during the election campaign and, at the end of June, produced an overwhelming victory for the Gaullist party, rechristened Union for the Defence of the Republic (UDR). Although de Gaulle received credit for having pulled himself and the country together on 30 May, the election was widely perceived as Pompidou's victory, not the General's.

For de Gaulle the resolution had come at a very high price. The events of May had not initially been motivated by hostility to him, but once they had begun he naturally became a prime target. Worse still, over the course of the month many hitherto well-disposed citizens and politicians demonstrably lost faith in his leadership and transferred their allegiance to Pompidou. At the end de Gaulle had only been able to reassert his leadership by pandering to the fears of the 'party of order', by abandoning the ecumenical role that he had tried to play on 24 May, and by postponing the dialogue between General de Gaulle and the people in favour of a partisan contest between the Gaullist party and the other parties. He had done it because he knew that he had no other option, but it was clearly a last resort.

De Gaulle's main preoccupation in the eleven months that separated the May events from his resignation at the end of April 1969 was to repair this damage to his own authority and to that of the regime. He began by accepting Pompidou's resignation (which at the last moment the latter tried to retract) and by appointing the unspectacular but loyal Couve de Murville in his place. This was, in a sense, a replay of April 1962, when Debré had been dropped as soon as the Algerian crisis had been resolved. In both cases, there were those who accused the president of ingratitude or even of resenting the political strength of his prime minister. In Pompidou's case, unlike in Debré's, the parting precipitated a rapid and rather bitter falling-out between the president and his former prime minister.

Pompidou's replacement gained de Gaulle some freedom of manoeuvre, but it did nothing to allay the apprehensions of Gaullist politicians, who feared that the General was determined to return to his disastrous participation schemes. These fears proved fully justified. After the 'revolution' of 1968, as in the aftermath of the liberation, de Gaulle was determined not to confuse the restoration of public order and political stability with a simple return to the status quo ante. He accepted the widespread view that the regime's immobility in the Pompidou years had contributed to the outbreak of the crisis. As soon as it was over he took to the television screens (7 June) to emphasize that he had not given up the constructive reform ideas that he had expressed on 24 May. When the new education minister, Edgar Faure, proposed a radical reform of higher education, de Gaulle stood by the plan, even though in some respects it differed from his own preferences and encountered harsh criticism from the right wing of the UDR.

Two of the fundamental principles in Faure's plan, which became law in the autumn of 1968, were greater autonomy for the universities and a new system of governance involving elected councils composed of students and teachers. These principles were in line with three other initiatives that de Gaulle unveiled in a confidential note to ministers at the end of July 1968.[25] At the national level, he proposed to replace the Senate with a new consultative body composed of locally and regionally elected representatives and representatives of the major social and economic interest groups. At the regional level, he proposed to devolve significant powers to a network of new regional councils. Finally, in the workplace, he proposed legislation to give all employees the right to be kept informed of their company's performance, to play a role in important decisions, and to have a financial stake in company profits.

This note, which was subsequently leaked to the newspaper *Le Figaro*, also contained the startling news that de Gaulle had given up the idea of putting the principle of worker participation to a popular vote. Only the first two issues – Senate reform and regionalization – would be decided by referendum. Worker participation could be enacted by simple legislation. Why de Gaulle should have stepped back so soon from his earlier commitment and focussed the referendum on two less important issues is not clear. It was certainly not that he was backing away from participation itself: he continued to lobby for it in every televised appearance, as well as in his last press conference in September 1968. The minister who was in charge of participation reform, Jean-Marcel Jeanneney, suggested that de Gaulle came round to the view that such a fundamental restructuring of industrial relations would take a long time to prepare and that it would be premature to submit it to a popular vote in a matter of months.[26] Another explanation is the tactical one: putting on the ballot an issue that was regarded by Pompidou, by most Gaullist deputies, by employers, and by some members of his own government as the first step towards sovietization would have made it very easy for them to betray him. However deeply held his belief in the flaws of unreconstructed capitalism, the record of his public career suggests that he did not view worker participation as one of those fundamental principles on which there could be no compromise. His first priority after May 1968 was to restore the current of confidence between himself and his people. In other words it was more important to have a referendum than to have it on the issue of worker participation.

There was an undeniably tragic air to this period after the May events, as some of de Gaulle's most hard-fought and prized achievements unravelled. In August 1968 the arrival of Soviet troops in Czechoslovakia dealt a fatal blow to his grand international design. At home, the currency reserves that he had been building up since the beginning of his republic dissipated in a matter of months, as Couve de Murville's government was forced to pump money into the economy to restore business confidence and to honour the agreements that Pompidou had reached with the trade unions in May 1968. This surge of spending soon put the franc under pressure, and by the autumn devaluation appeared all but certain. On political grounds de Gaulle refused to devalue, but he could only avoid it by ordering severe cuts in government expenditure. Among the programmes whose budget was reduced was that for nuclear testing. There could hardly have been a more telling symbol of the limitations on what was still, after a decade of Gaullist *grandeur*, a medium-sized power.

Above all, there was something tragic about the manner in which de Gaulle pressed on towards a final confrontation with the electorate which seemed increasingly likely to go against him. A stream of visitors to the Elysée urged him to put off the referendum or at any rate to split up the two questions, since the regional reform was popular, while the Senate reform immediately ran into criticism. But in the end postponement was unthinkable, because it would have meant betraying his own method, giving up the hope of a renewed connection between himself and the French people. At the beginning of February 1969 he announced that the referendum would be held in the spring. Later in the month the Council of Ministers fixed the date: 27 April 1969. De Gaulle made it clear that, as in past referenda, he would regard anything less than a clear endorsement as automatically terminating his mission.

Some have described the referendum as a political suicide, but that is perhaps too straightforward. If de Gaulle had wanted to resign, he could have done so without the pretext of a referendum.[27] If this was a suicide, it was a partially involuntary one. In effect, de Gaulle was attempting to repeat one last time the feat of political acrobatics which he had been performing throughout the Fifth Republic – the feat of holding on to conservative support while reaching out to the rest of the nation as a progressive reformer, of being both partisan and non-partisan at the same time. After the shock of May 1968 he knew that he might fail (which probably only added to the appeal of the enterprise) but he also believed, until close to the end, that he had a chance of pulling it off. The odds were stacked against him for two reasons: first because conservatives were no longer afraid to let him go, once Pompidou had declared his intention to run for president, as he did in January 1969; and, second, because those outside the Gaullist party were reluctant to extend a hand to him – because the memories of his role in the reaction of June 1968 were still fresh in their minds, because they were unimpressed by his paternalistic rhetoric about participation, or perhaps simply because they were tired of being blackmailed by his 'me or chaos' line. In the end there was no groundswell of opinion to force the General out. There was simply no groundswell to keep him in office on his terms.

The result of the referendum was 47.5 per cent in favour and 52.5 per cent against. At midnight on 27 April 1969 de Gaulle issued a communiqué to the effect that he would cease to be president at noon the following day. He remained in seclusion in Colombey for a couple of weeks, before leaving for an extended vacation in Ireland. There he began work on the final great labour of his life, writing his second set of memoirs. The first volume of the *Memoirs of Hope* appeared in October 1970. Two weeks later, on 9 November, he died suddenly at home. In accordance with a will that he had drawn up in 1952, he was buried in the cemetery at Colombey beside his daughter Anne in the presence of family, close friends, wartime comrades, and villagers. As he had stipulated, no representative of the French government or of foreign governments attended the funeral. The inscription on his headstone read simply: 'Charles de Gaulle, 1890–1970'. Years before, in one of his notebooks, he had recorded a quotation from one of his favourite authors, Chateaubriand: 'Il faut de grands tombeaux aux petits hommes et de petits tombeaux aux grands.'[28]

. . .

NOTES AND REFERENCES

1. Flohic F 1979 *Souvenirs d'outre-Gaulle.* Plon, Paris, p. 172.
2. Speech of 31/12/68, DM vol. 5 p. 357.
3. Lacouture J 1986 *De Gaulle* (3 vols). Le Seuil, Paris, vol. 3 p. 760.
4. Viansson-Ponté P 1971 *Histoire de la république gaullienne.* Laffont, Paris, p. 586.
5. Boissieu A de 1982 *Pour servir le général 1946–1970.* Plon, Paris, p. 176.
6. Pompidou G 1982 *Pour rétablir une vérité.* Flammarion, Paris, p. 191.
7. Rouanet A, Rouanet P 1980 *Les Trois Derniers Chagrins du Général de Gaulle.* Grasset, Paris, pp. 238–9.
8. Rouanet A, P 1980 pp. 209, 218–20.
9. LNC vol. 11 p. 219.

10. Aron R 1969 *The Elusive Revolution* trans G Clough. Praeger, New York, p. 33.
11. Dansette A 1971 *Mai 1968*. Plon, Paris, pp. 248–9.
12. Boissieu A de 1982 p. 181; Rouanet A, P 1980 p. 267.
13. Bénéton P, Touchard J 1970 Les Interprétations de la crise de mai-juin 1968. *Revue française de science politique*, **20** (3): 542n.
14. Lacouture J 1986 vol. 3 p. 690.
15. Pompidou G 1982 p. 190.
16. Pompidou G 1982 p. 191.
17. Massu J 1983 *Baden 68*. Plon, Paris.
18. Pompidou G 1982 p. 201.
19. Flohic F 1979 pp. 176-84; Boissieu A de 1982 pp. 185–91.
20. Massu J 1983 pp. 103–4, 152.
21. Boissieu A de 1982 p. 185.
22. 7/6/68, DM vol. 5 p. 295.
23. Aron R 1969 p. 25.
24. Hoffmann S 1974 Confrontation in May 1968, *Decline or Renewal? France since the 1930s*. Viking, New York, p. 168.
25. LNC vol. 11 pp. 232–3.
26. Lacouture J 1986 vol. 3 p. 740.
27. D'Escrienne J 1973 *Le Général m'a dit . . . 1966–1970*. Plon, Paris, pp. 47–8 .
28. LNC vol. 12 p. 181.

CONCLUSION

Léon Blum, France's first socialist prime minister, once described Charles de Gaulle as a kind of pessimist whose scorn for human beings prevented him from believing in the usefulness of any action but who nonetheless felt an overwhelming compulsion to act.[1] Blum put his finger on an important complexity in de Gaulle's character. This quintessential man of action, who twice took it upon himself to rescue his country from disaster and dishonour, was also a sceptic who believed that 'things have been the same since the world has been the world', as he told Richard Nixon.[2] This republican monarch, who gave France a new constitution and exercised greater power than any political figure in France's modern history, was always burdened by an acute sense of the limits on his action – the weaknesses and divisions of his people, the unalterable realities of the historical conjuncture in which he had to operate, and the ultimate limit of his own mortality, which, having entered public life at a relatively advanced age, he felt with special keenness. This patriot who never tired of urging France to be herself and of holding out an exceptional destiny for her spent much of his career waiting for the nuclear apocalypse of World War III or fretting over France's national decline.

But on one point Blum was mistaken. Except in his blackest moments, de Gaulle was a sceptic, not a fatalist. He acted not just out of compulsion, but because he firmly believed in his own ability to overcome fate. At the root of everything de Gaulle did after 1940 was the ambition that he had revealed in *The Edge of the Sword*, the ambition to leave his mark on history by playing a great role in great events.

A career conceived in these lofty terms deserves to be judged by similarly high standards. For three decades de Gaulle was a towering figure in French politics and a substantial figure in international politics. He presided over profound transformations in France's socio-economic structure, in the relations of the French with one another and with other peoples. But the 'second French revolution' of economic modernization, the global transformation of decolonization, and the collapse of discredited political regimes in France would all have happened, even if de Gaulle had served out his career in the army. The further de Gaulle's career recedes into history, the more distinctly two moments in it stand out from the rest. At these two points his individual intervention had a decisive and lasting impact on the course of French history.

The first came, of course, during the German Occupation. In the French collective memory, General de Gaulle is chiefly remembered as the first resister and the national liberator. There is an element of legend here: he created *a* Resistance but not *the* Resistance, and in military terms his organization played a minor role in the liberation. There is, though, a larger element of truth. De Gaulle's actions between 1940 and 1944 did indeed shape the conditions under which the French people experienced liberation – that is to say, as a relatively orderly, broadly consensual take-over supervised by a French government that was widely regarded as legitimate both inside and outside the country. In the process de Gaulle averted two alternative scenarios (both perfectly plausible in the circumstances): either a popular uprising, which might well have led to bitter civil conflict; or a behind-the-scenes deal involving Vichy, the Allies, and perhaps an improvised French authority, which would have cast a prolonged shadow over France's international standing and might well have produced a popular backlash. The merits of the resolution that de Gaulle orchestrated have not gone without challenge, particularly from those who supported Vichy or from resisters who aspired to a genuine social revolution and resented (understandably) the General's apparent contempt for their contribution to liberation. On the other hand, it can hardly be doubted that de Gaulle's actions helped to restore national unity, revived France's international prestige, and in general eased the transition to the postwar era.

The second intervention fourteen years later had an equally profound impact. In 1958 he harnessed the enormous pressure that had built up as a result of the war in Algeria to break the constitutional impasse that France had been enduring since the early 1930s. Then, by covering the new regime with his personal prestige and authority, he gave it time to sink roots in the nation and in the body politic, while he engineered a relatively swift and successful disengagement from Algeria and from the empire in general. Even if decolonization, like liberation, was inevitable, it was not inevitable in the manner in which it occurred. Without de Gaulle the process would almost certainly have been more protracted and wrenching, and in all likelihood would have involved France in full-scale civil war. Finally, in the constitutional revision of 1962, he consummated the transition from an old parliamentary republicanism to a new presidentialism.

In both these critical phases of de Gaulle's career, the key to his successful intervention was the set of intuitions about himself and the world that he had carried with him for many years. These intuitions, which one might term Gaullist myths, allowed him to find his bearings amid complex and constantly shifting events, to construct large simplifications about the meaning of these events, and to identify a personal role for himself in them. In other words, the myths lay at the root of what was most distinctive and fundamental to his leadership: an enormous lucidity about history and his own part in it.

Two myths, in particular, formed the basis of de Gaulle's world-view. One was the myth of the man of character, first expressed in *The Edge of the Sword*, the book which was 'a self-portrait in anticipation'.[3] It reads like a fairy tale. Once upon a time there was a soldier who had all the gifts of character and intellect to be a leader, but was too independent and proud to be popular with his colleagues and subordinates. While his country was enjoying peace, he was passed over by his superiors, who preferred to promote more docile and accommodating soldiers with lesser talents. Suddenly the country was struck by a great disaster. All the lesser leaders fell away and the whole country spontaneously rallied to greatness. Spurred on by his taste for responsibility and his relish for difficult challenges, the man of character assumed sole command. As a leader, he relied not on rank or hierarchy, but on his personal prestige, maintained through a combination of carefully calculated aloofness and well-timed, highly theatrical interventions. To galvanize his followers, he set them only the most ambitious goals; he exuded contempt for lesser ambitions. All the while, however, this consummate performer was also keeping a keen eye for contingencies and modifying his policy as circumstances required.

The other seminal Gaullist myth concerned France and the world. This was the myth of an old country, once the most powerful of all nations and still, for all its travails, uniquely revered and influential. In a dangerous world full of envious and predatory rivals, this country had reached a crossroads in its history. In one direction lay the downward-sloping and inviting path of *facilité* – the attitude of accepting national mediocrity and dependence on others. This path led inexorably to decline. In the other direction rose a steep and arduous road that led to *grandeur*. Only by opting for the high road could France remain true to herself, but the temptations of the low road and the vulnerabilities of the French people, who at any one moment constituted the living embodiment of France, created the condition for a perpetual national drama.

Guiding France towards the high road were three fundamental imperatives. The first was the principle of renewal, which signified the necessity constantly to adapt to changed circumstances. To de Gaulle, renewal was almost a law of nature. As he wrote in 1934: 'No enterprise lasts without continual renovation.'[4] His entire career might be described as an extended application of this principle. The thrust of his inter-war activity was to compel the French army to adapt to the new conditions of mechanized warfare. After the liberation he championed the cause of social, economic, and political renewal. In the late 1950s and early 1960s he presented decolonization as a form of renewal, bringing France into harmony with new global realities. In the same period he urged France, in a famous expression, 'to marry her century', to embrace the technological and industrial order of the late-twentieth century. From his earliest years to the end of his life, de Gaulle believed in the imperative of change. Though he immersed himself in history and was not immune to nostalgic evocations of an earlier and simpler age, he believed that a living nation could only, by definition, live in the present.

If renewal was a law of nature, the autonomy of the nation-state was the highest law of nations. In de Gaulle's view, nations were the only enduring realities in the world. When strange supranational apparitions such as the Cominform or the European Defence Community broke into his fairy-tale landscape, de Gaulle was always sure that, beneath the elaborate disguise of ideology, lurked the familiar figure of nations pursuing their interests. To be herself – in other words to be true to her nature as a nation – France had to retain her independence. Any act that jeopardized or surrendered it – whether it involved signing an armistice with a national enemy or basing one's policy on that of a foreign power or integrating French military forces under a non-French command – was not just wrong. It was, to use a word from his memoirs, absurd.

The third law – the law of unity – was neither a law of nature nor a law of nations, but a law that pertained specifically to the French nation. In de Gaulle's myth, a fundamental characteristic of France was its inner fragmentation. In an immediate sense this was associated with the century and a half of intermittent civil conflict that France had experienced since 1789. In a more profound way, however, fragmentation was part of the very essence of France, something which had marked the nation from its beginnings in late antiquity. It was the reason why France was compelled always to aim for the summits: only the continual pursuit of grandeur could, by mobilizing consensus, counteract this tragic flaw. It was also the reason that France needed a strong centralized state and had always needed one. Without a strong state the country would lapse back into a feudal chaos of competing classes and cliques. De Gaulle cast France's history in Tocquevillian terms. Its fundamental conflict was not the relatively recent one between the revolution and its enemies, but the ancient one between state-builders (Henri IV, Richelieu,

Napoleon, de Gaulle) and the feudal opponents of the
state (nobilities of the ancien régime implicitly equated
with the latter-day 'barons' of the political parties, the trade
unions, and the press).

The two myths (of the man of character and of the
unique status of France) constituted not so much an ideology – although for Gaullists they performed this function
– but rather a set of highly personalized and imaginative
intuitions about 'how things are', about how human beings
and nations in general, and General de Gaulle and France
in particular, must act. The factual accuracy of the myths
(an issue that naturally obsessed the General's opponents)
was of secondary importance, at any rate in periods of
extreme crisis. The fact was that in moments like those,
when the French world or the wider world seemed in flux
and no longer comprehensible by the old standards, de
Gaulle's ability to appeal to these myths gave him an
almost insuperable authority and appeal.

That is not to say that the myths were enough to guarantee
success. The man of character only succeeded in 1940–44
and 1958–62 because he also developed into a skilled
politician. In both periods, as we have seen, he showed a
remarkable ability to adapt his organization and modify his
message in order to advance his cause. What is striking
about these periods is how comfortably he was able to
combine the roles of mythic hero and political leader.

Of course, that was easier to do in wartime, when the
presence of a national emergency 'covered', in a sense, the
political decisions that he had to make. In a curious way,
the greater challenge for a leader like de Gaulle, who for
most of his adult life concentrated his thoughts and
energies on the problem of how to deal with situations of
extreme danger, was to adapt to the absence of crisis. His
achievements as a crisis leader can scarcely be questioned,
but his record outside the two great crises leaves much
more room for debate and disagreement.

In many respects he adapted remarkably well – far
better, for example, than Churchill. By 1962 he had
achieved, albeit after a long and tortuous process, an
institutional arrangement that gave him the political support
that he needed without undermining the ecumenical status
he craved. It is difficult to conceive of a more effective

institutionalization of crisis leadership than the presidency of the Fifth Republic. His adaptation to 'normal' times was also aided by the reformist instinct, which ran throughout his career and which gave a purposeful and constructive air to his reign. His historical reputation will probably not rest primarily on his reformist achievements, but they were considerable, both in the much maligned liberation government and in the Fifth Republic years.

On the other hand, in spite of these successes, it can be argued that de Gaulle's leadership tended to run into the sand outside periods of crisis. In peacetime a general plans for the next war, but can a political leader continually plan for the next crisis? De Gaulle's inclination was to do so. Or rather, equating normality with mediocrity, he sought to perpetuate a sense that France was living through a period of epic challenge. This technique helped to push the pace of economic modernization and to develop an assertive foreign policy. It was particularly effective with the generation that had experienced defeat in 1940. But, psychologically and politically, it was a difficult strategy to sustain. Sooner or later, people were bound to weary of being marched from one 'battle' to another, of being constantly confronted by the stark alternative between *grandeur* and disaster.

Equally problematic was de Gaulle's emphasis on unity and the unifying role of the leader and the state. He conceived of himself and his state as guardians of the larger interest of eternal France and, as such, socially and politically impartial. In conditions other than those of crisis, however, such an assumption was questionable. His own attitudes and policies inevitably appealed to certain segments of the population more than to others. Politically, he depended on the support of a Gaullist party, which had a strongly partisan bias. In 1944–58 and again after 1962 this placed him in a difficult position. If he reverted to the consensual role of the saviour in conditions that did not appear to call for a saviour, he risked marginalizing himself. If he accepted the practical necessity of partisanship outside crisis, he demystified himself. As we have seen, his preference (at any rate after the disappointments of 1944–46) was for the second option. This strategy worked in the short term, but it had its price, as the final phase of his career demonstrated.

A society is not an army, but de Gaulle often treated French society as though it were. The charge that he was fundamentally undemocratic – often made in the RPF period and again in the late 1960s – misses the point. He was self-evidently a democrat in the sense that he recognized that, in the circumstances of the mid-twentieth century, the French state could only rest on popular consent. But he was a democrat with a very heavily instrumental view of politics. He saw politics as a form of mobilization, not as a participatory process. Although he talked a good deal about participation, what he meant by this was a system in which individuals or groups were willing to transcend their differences and unite for a common effort. There were obviously times when such mobilization for a common effort was called for. But when it became a perpetual and all-consuming imperative, it became stifling, especially as people sensed that the direction of their common effort was being set in authoritarian style from above.

As a result of problems such as these, by the end of his reign de Gaulle's leadership had become harder for the French people to tolerate. The fact that they now appreciate it less grudgingly, at least to judge by opinion polls conducted twenty years after his death, shows perhaps that it is easier to live with mythic leaders when they are dead than when they are alive.

· · ·

NOTES AND REFERENCES

1. Blum L 1955 *L'Oeuvre de Léon Blum* (9 vols). Albin Michel, Paris, vol. 5 (1940–1945), p. 114.
2. Alphand H 1977 *L'Etonnement d'être*. Fayard, Paris, p. 398.
3. Hoffmann S 1974 De Gaulle as Political Artist: The Will to Grandeur, *Decline or Renewal? France since the 1930s*. Viking, New York, p. 217.
4. De Gaulle C 1934 *Vers l'armée de métier*. Berger-Levrault, Paris, p. 47.

BIBLIOGRAPHICAL ESSAY

The natural starting-point for anyone studying de Gaulle is his own writing. The three volumes of *Mémoires de guerre* (War Memoirs) are indispensable for the period 1940–46. They are also the best source for de Gaulle's world-view and for the mythic identity that he forged for himself. They are available in translation: 1955 *Call to Honour: 1940–42* trans J Griffin, Collins; 1959 *Unity: 1942–44* trans R Howard, Weidenfeld and Nicolson; 1960 *Salvation: 1944–46* trans R Howard, Weidenfeld and Nicolson. However, the full effect of de Gaulle's superbly crafted classical style and romantic temper can only be appreciated in the original (1954–59 Plon, Paris). The second set of memoirs, 1970 *Mémoires d'espoir*, was left unfinished at his death. These memoirs too are available in translation: 1971 *Memoirs of Hope* trans T Kilmartin, Weidenfeld and Nicolson. The first volume, *Renewal*, is valuable for the period 1958–62, although its tone is even more serene than that of the *War Memoirs*; it is history written for the benefit of posterity, without flaws, uncertainties or mistakes. He completed just two chapters of the second volume, *Endeavour*.

Historians have always paid considerable attention to de Gaulle's prewar writing, particularly 1960 *The Edge of the Sword* trans G Hopkins, Faber and Faber and Criterion Books, New York, and 1940 *The Army of the Future* Hutchinson. Of more immediate relevance to his political career are the two multi-volume collections of his papers (neither available in English). The five volumes of his speeches and addresses, 1970 *Discours et messages* Plon, Paris, were compiled under his supervision shortly before his death. They

166

contain most of his major public pronouncements, although there are some interesting omissions (such as the speech in which he uttered, for the one and only time, the words 'Vive l'Algérie française!'). Recently, his son Philippe has supervised the publication of twelve volumes of papers from the General's archives, 1980–88 *Lettres, notes et carnets* Plon, Paris. These volumes contain material from every stage of de Gaulle's life. They are particularly illuminating for the early years and for the period of the Second World War. On the other hand, apart from occasional revelations, they are much less useful for the Fifth Republic period. One should also note that, since de Gaulle reportedly wrote 150,000 letters, the published material represents only a small sample. The remainder of his private archives remain closed to researchers. So do the public archives from the years after 1958. This introduces an inescapable imbalance into the historical writing about de Gaulle, since historians now have access to extensive archival material for the Free France years, the post-liberation era, and the RPF, and yet must still rely heavily upon memoirs and journalistic sources for the entire Fifth Republic period.

The literature about de Gaulle is intimidating in terms of sheer quantity. There are now almost 2,000 books about him, not to mention numerous articles, scholarly or otherwise. The last decade, in particular, has seen a remarkable flowering of 'Gaullian' studies. An international bibliography produced by the Institut Charles de Gaulle lists 1,700 new entries for the decade 1980–90. As recently as 1981, Professor Douglas Johnson could comment, with some justification, on the large gaps in our knowledge about de Gaulle. Recent scholarship has filled many, though by no means all, of these gaps.

We now have a comprehensive and convincing biography: J Lacouture 1984–86 *De Gaulle* (3 vols) Le Seuil, Paris. Lacouture wrote a short and rather critical biography in the 1960s, but like many of his generation his view of the General seems to have mellowed with the passage of time. His second effort is not only far longer than the first, but far more appreciative of de Gaulle's achievements and sympathetic to his personality. Until de Gaulle's archives and government archives become fully available, this will remain the definitive biography. The English translation

(1990–91 Collins) unfortunately compresses the final two volumes into a single one, but is still invaluable. It may be supplemented by two shorter but able biographical treatments: B Ledwidge 1982 *De Gaulle* Weidenfeld and Nicolson; and J Jackson 1990 *Charles de Gaulle* Cardinal. For those who read French, a wealth of biographical material is contained in the journal of the Institut Charles de Gaulle, *Espoir*, which appears four times a year, and in a magazine entitled *En ce temps-là de Gaulle*, which was published by Editions du Hénin between 1971 and 1973. Many of the anecdotes that have been recycled again and again in biographies of the General were first brought to light by the journalist Jean-Raymond Tournoux, who published a series of books including 1966 *Pétain and de Gaulle* trans O Coburn, Heinemann and Viking, New York, and 1971 *Jamais dit* Plon, Paris.

The last decade has also produced a number of important memoirs by close associates of the General. Particularly useful (for different phases of his career) are Michel Debré 1984–88 *Mémoires* (3 vols) Albin Michel, Paris; Alain de Boissieu 1982 *Pour servir le général 1946–1970* Plon, Paris; Louis Terrenoire 1981 *De Gaulle 1947–1954: pourquoi l'échec?* Plon, Paris; and Gaston Palewski 1988 *Mémoires d'action 1924–1974* Plon, Paris. These supplement earlier memoirs such as those by Hervé Alphand 1977 *L'Etonnement d'être* Fayard, Paris; Maurice Couve de Murville 1971 *Une politique étrangère 1958–1969* Plon, Paris; Bernard Tricot 1972 *Les Sentiers de la paix. Algérie 1958–1962* Plon, Paris; Olivier Guichard 1980 *Mon général* Grasset, Paris; Claude Mauriac 1978 *Le Temps immobile: aimer de Gaulle* Grasset, Paris (an earlier version of which appeared in English: 1973 *The Other de Gaulle. Diaries, 1944–1954* trans M Budberg, G Latta, Angus and Robertson). A fragmentary memoir by Georges Pompidou was published posthumously in 1982: *Pour rétablir une vérité* Flammarion, Paris. It contains interesting material about the RPF years and about 1968, although its account of the May crisis and aftermath is seriously flawed.

One of the most distinctive and creative areas of 'Gaullology' has been the organized collaboration between those who worked with the General and those who study his career from an academic standpoint. Over the past fifteen years the Institut Charles de Gaulle in Paris has convened a series of conferences which have combined scholarly presentations (often of a very high calibre) with first-hand recollections by the General's associates, ministers, and aides. Though the published records of these conferences are often rather dense and inaccessible to the non-expert, not to mention couched in excessively reverential terms, they contain many insights, both into de Gaulle's exercise of power and into various aspects of his policy. For his exercise of power, three volumes are particularly important: 1990 *De Gaulle et ses premiers ministres* Plon, Paris; 1979 *'L'Entourage' et de Gaulle* Plon, Paris; 1977 *De Gaulle et le service de l'Etat* Plon, Paris. The conferences on specific areas of policy are now too numerous to list, but mention should be made of the 'super-conference' that was held during the centenary celebrations in 1990. The records of that event are to be published by Plon and La Documentation Française under the title *De Gaulle en son siècle* (6 vols). The first volume, *Dans la mémoire des hommes et des peuples*, appeared in 1991.

The last decade has produced a new generation of authoritative monographs, which have been able to take advantage of the increasing accessibility of archival sources for the period up to 1958. François Kersaudy has given a thorough and elegant account of de Gaulle's war years in 1982 *Churchill and de Gaulle* Collins and Atheneum, New York. On the RPF there are two outstanding studies, both of which are based on archives in the Institut Charles de Gaulle. Jean Charlot 1983 *Le Gaullisme d'opposition 1946–1958* Fayard, Paris is a model of clarity and precision. P Guiol 1985 *L'Impasse sociale du gaullisme: Le RPF et l'action ouvrière* Presses de la FNSP, Paris is an important study of de Gaulle's labour-capital association idea. On de Gaulle's return in 1958 René Rémond has written a brief but incisive account: 1983 *Le Retour de de Gaulle* Editions Complexe, Brussels; and Odile Rudelle has written a longer study based on archives and interviews: 1988 *Mai 58: De Gaulle et la République* Plon, Paris. Nothing comparable to these works has yet been written about the 1960s, although there are a number of excellent studies of de Gaulle's foreign policy in that period, including P Cerny 1980 *The Politics of Grandeur: Ideological Aspects of de Gaulle's Foreign Policy* Cambridge, and E Kolodziej 1974 *French International Policy under de Gaulle and Pompidou: The Politics of Grandeur* Cornell UP, Ithaca. For the domestic picture in the 1960s the most reliable guides are still P Williams and M Harrison 1971 *Politics and Society in de Gaulle's Republic* Longman and Doubleday, New York (1973); and P Viansson-Ponté 1971 *Histoire de la république gaullienne* Laffont, Paris. J-P Guichard 1985 *De Gaulle et les mass media* France-Empire, Paris is an informative analysis of de Gaulle's use of modern communications techniques.

On Gaullism Jean Touchard wrote a remarkably astute study in 1978 *Le Gaullisme 1940–1969* Le Seuil, Paris. There are also some excellent observations in D Johnson 1965 The Political Principles of General de Gaulle, *International Affairs*, 41: 650–62. The evolution of the Gaullist movement in the 1960s is discussed in J Charlot 1971 *The Gaullist Phenomenon* trans M Charlot and M Neighbour, Allen and Unwin.

For insights that range beyond particular periods or policies, the essays of Stanley Hoffmann are in a class of their own. Most of the important ones can be found in 1974 *Decline or Renewal? France since the 1930s* Viking, New York. They may be complemented by the work of two great French writers. F Mauriac 1966 *De Gaulle* trans R Howard, Bodley Head offers a perceptive, if indulgent, interpretation. The other classic is A Malraux 1972 *Fallen Oaks* trans I Clephane, Hamilton. Malraux's book is an account of his last meeting with de Gaulle in December 1969. It is not certain how many of the *obiter dicta* that Malraux attributed to de Gaulle were actually said, but the book conveys many larger, if not literal, truths about its subject. A recent book which also deals with de Gaulle's last years and which may well acquire the status of a classic is: P-L Blanc 1990 *De Gaulle au soir de sa vie* Fayard, Paris. Blanc assisted de Gaulle in the preparation of the *Memoirs of Hope* and gives a sensitive and revealing portrait of the man behind the myth.

CHRONOLOGY

1890	Born in Lille, 22 November
1900	Enters Jesuit school in Paris
1910	Enters the military school at Saint-Cyr
1912	Graduates from Saint-Cyr; joins 33rd infantry regiment commanded by Colonel Pétain
1914	Wounded in action two weeks after beginning of First World War
1915	Promoted to captain; wounded again in action
1916	Wounded in the Battle of Verdun; taken prisoner
1918	Released from prison at the end of the war; returned to France
1919–20	Serves as instructor in Polish military academy; sees action against the Red Army
1921	Appointed lecturer in history at Saint-Cyr; marries Yvonne Vendroux; birth of first child, Philippe
1922	Enters War College
1924	Publishes first book, *La Discorde chez l'ennemi*; birth of second child, Elisabeth; completes War College course
1927	Delivers three lectures on leadership at the War College
1928	Birth of third child, Anne
1929	Leaves for two-year posting in Beirut
1931	Posted to Secretariat of the Supreme Council for National Defence in Paris
1932	Death of his father, Henri de Gaulle; publishes second book, *Le Fil de l'épée*

1934   Publishes third book, *Vers l'armée de métier*; purchases 'La Boisserie', his house at Colombey-les-Deux-Eglises; meets Paul Reynaud, who agrees to publicize his proposals for a motorized, professional army

1936   Meets with Léon Blum, head of Popular Front government, but fails to persuade him to back motorized army

1937   Takes command of 507th tank regiment in Metz; promoted to colonel

1938   Publishes fourth book, *La France et son armée*; breaks off relations with Pétain

1939   France and Britain declare war on Germany

1940   Sends memorandum to eighty military and civilian leaders urging creation of a mechanized force; German invasion of Low Countries and France; promoted to brigadier-general; appointed Under-Secretary for National Defence; flies to London and broadcasts 'appel' of 18 June; Third Republic replaced by Pétain's 'Etat Français' in Vichy; recognized by the British government as head of the Free French; death of his mother, Jeanne de Gaulle (née Maillot); condemned to death for desertion by a Vichy military court; Dakar fiasco; creates Council of Imperial Defence

1941   Crisis in relations with British precipitated by events in Syria and Lebanon; USSR and USA enter war against Axis powers

1942   Sends Moulin into France to unify resistance; Free French victory at Bir Hakeim; 'declaration' of 23 June published in clandestine newspapers inside France; Free France renamed Fighting France; American landings in North Africa; Vichyite Darlan recognized by Americans as High Commissioner of French North Africa; after Darlan's assassination, Giraud appointed as replacement

1943   Forced to meet with Giraud in presence of Churchill and Roosevelt at Casablanca; receives backing from National Council of the Resistance; reaches agreement with Giraud to form French Committee of National Liberation; flies to

Algiers; convenes Consultative Assembly; marginalizes Giraud

1944 Brazzaville Conference; Allied landings in Normandy; first trip to liberated France, 14 June; received by Roosevelt at the White House; Paris liberated, 25 August; heads triumphant procession down the Champs-Elysées, 26 August; transfers provisional government from Algiers to Paris; tours provinces to ensure smooth transfer of power; provisional government recognized by Allies; meeting with Stalin in Moscow

1945 End of war; excluded from Allied conferences at Yalta and Potsdam; introduces major domestic reforms; referendum and elections for Constituent Assembly; elected by Constituent Assembly to head government

1946 Resigns from government; first constitutional draft rejected by electorate; Bayeux speech outlines Gaullist constitution; second constitutional draft approved by electorate over de Gaulle's opposition

1947 Fourth Republic officially founded; forms Rassemblement du Peuple Français; communist ministers dismissed from the government; announcement of Marshall Plan; huge RPF success in municipal elections

1948 Death of daughter Anne

1949 NATO founded

1951 RPF wins 119 seats in legislative elections

1952 Split in RPF parliamentary group; attacks European Defence Community

1953 Begins to wind up RPF

1954 Defeat of French army in Indochina at Dien Bien Phu; end of war in Indochina; European Defence Community voted down by French parliament; publication of first volume of *Mémoires de guerre*, 100,000 copies sold in five weeks; nationalist rebellion breaks out in Algeria

1956 Abortive Anglo-French operation at Suez

1957 Signing of Treaties of Rome creating Euratom and the EEC

1958	Uprising in Algiers; returns to power with authority to draw up new constitution; 'Je vous ai compris' speech in Algiers; receives Adenauer at Colombey; memorandum to Eisenhower and Macmillan demands transformation of NATO; eighty per cent of voters approve constitution for the Fifth Republic; creation of the Gaullist UNR, which becomes largest parliamentary party after general elections in November; elected president by an electoral college of 80,000 notables; Rueff plan
1959	Common Market comes into effect; Fifth Republic officially founded; appoints Debré prime minister; withdraws French Mediterranean fleet from NATO command; 'self-determination' speech launches new Algerian initiative
1960	Barricades Week in Algiers; first French atomic explosion in the Sahara; hosts East-West summit in Paris; first negotiations with the rebel Algerian Provisional Government; acknowledges likelihood of Algerian independence in televised address; last visit to Algeria
1961	Referendum on Algerian self-determination finds seventy-five per cent in favour; creation of Fouchet Commission; Generals' *putsch* in Algiers; activates article 16 of constitution and assumes emergency powers; opening of negotiations at Evian; building of Berlin Wall; escapes OAS assassination attempt at Pont-sur-Seine
1962	Evian Accords signed and approved by voters; Debré replaced as prime minister by Pompidou; Fouchet plan rejected by France's EEC partners; escapes most serious assassination attempt at Petit-Clamart; Cuban Missile Crisis; referendum approves direct election of President of the Republic; UNR wins legislative elections
1963	Vetoes British entry into EEC and American proposal for Multilateral Nuclear Force; signs Franco-German treaty; bitter miners' strike; withdraws French Atlantic fleet from NATO command; pushes through stabilization plan to curb inflation; attends President Kennedy's funeral

1964 Recognizes People's Republic of China; undergoes prostate surgery; long visit to South America; signs Franco-Soviet commercial treaty

1965 Attends Churchill's funeral; attacks 'dollar hegemony'; adopts policy of 'empty chair' in Brussels; after months of speculation, announces decision to seek second presidential term; forced into run-off election against Mitterrand, but is re-elected with fifty-five per cent of the vote

1966 Announces decision to withdraw French forces from NATO command; agreement on Common Agricultural Policy ends French boycott in Brussels; visits to Soviet Union and Cambodia

1967 Legislative elections reduce Gaullist majority in parliament; second British application to join EEC rejected; Six Day War in the Middle East; controversial visit to French Canada; remarks at press conference interpreted as anti-Semitic

1968 US and North Vietnam begin negotiations in Paris; student uprisings spread from Nanterre to the Latin Quarter; goes ahead with planned visit to Romania; proposes referendum on participation; flight to Baden-Baden; radio address of 30 May restores order; Gaullist victory in legislative elections; Pompidou replaced as prime minister by Couve de Murville; Soviet intervention in Prague sets back Gaullist policy of *détente*; Faure's university reform approved by parliament; refuses to devalue franc

1969 Public split with Pompidou; 'Soames Affair', involving leaked reports of meeting between de Gaulle and British Ambassador in Paris, embitters relations with London; government proposal on regions and Senate is defeated in referendum and de Gaulle resigns; trip to Ireland; Pompidou elected to the presidency

1970 Publication of the *Discours et messages* and of the first volume of the *Mémoires d'espoir*; trip to Spain and meeting with Franco; dies at Colombey, 9 November; buried beside his daughter Anne, 12 November

MAPS

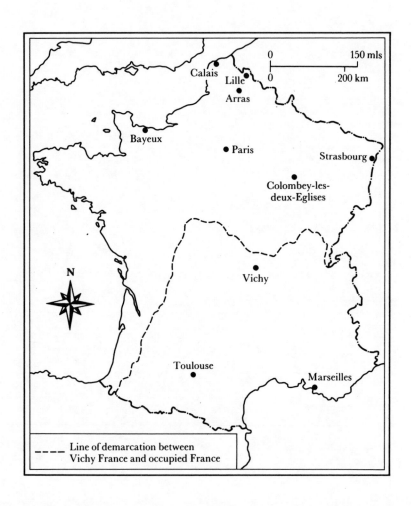

1. France showing the demarcation line, 1940–42

2. Algeria and the surrounding countries

3. Allied victory in Europe in the Second World War
After Felix Gilbert, *The End of the European Era, 1890 to the Present*
4th edition (London, 1991)

INDEX